MW00484546

My Guided Meditation

Using Meditation as a Therapeutic Tool to Focus Your Overactive Mind

Darcy Patrick

Edited by Samantha Green

My Guided Meditation
Copyright © 2019 by Darcy Patrick

All rights reserved. No part of this publication may be reproduced, distributed, or transmitted in any form or by any means, including photocopying, recording, or other electronic or mechanical methods, without the prior written permission of the author, except in the case of brief quotations embodied in critical reviews and certain other non-commercial uses permitted by copyright law.

Tellwell Talent
www.tellwell.ca

ISBN
978-0-2288-1328-6 (Paperback)
978-0-2288-1329-3 (eBook)

Cover Art by

Liz Chamberlain
www.lizzieloumixedmedia.com

Jennifer McCready
www.lady-luck-pinups.com

To learn more about Darcy Patrick, visit: www.darcypatrick.com

Table of Contents

Foreword

My Guided Meditation is book number three in a series of books that were inspired over the last 5 years since I started therapy for depression. I honestly had no idea that my life was going to take the turn it has taken since I walked into my first therapy session. Writing this meditation book has been a labor of love since I started. I chose to write all three of my books for one reason, and that is to help people like myself who struggled with depression, anxiety and mental health issues. These books and tools are not just meant for those people, but rather they are meant for everyone. We are all human and we all feel the same inside. I knew that if I found a way to show people what I went through, what I learned and how to succeed, I could help in ways I never originally thought possible. Shine a light and give hope, make a difference in people's lives, and hopefully prevent deaths – this has become my goal.

After my first book "Why I Run" was released, I discovered something from its success and the people I met. I discovered that all the years I spent trying to fit in and seeking approval from others was a learning experience, because being myself was enough. It turned out that doing my own thing without questioning it or caring what people thought, I was able to help people and reach them in ways that were unique to me. I was able to be at ground level and make an impact in people's lives, which I like to refer to as "digging in the dirt". My style of doing my own thing was to just be honest and write the way I wanted to write, not let anything influence me or change my way of thinking. This way of thinking, this mind set, powered me through writing this guided meditation book that you now hold in your hands. I believed in what I was writing and I believed in my way doing it and delivering results.

I wrote this book using the same style and techniques I used writing "Why I Run". I wrote as I worked on my meditation skills. I wrote with honesty and love for what I was doing, and shared my progress with others. I believed in what I was writing, because it was working for me. Guided meditation became a part of my life slowly; just like when I started therapy five years ago, I took my time and I learned to apply every tool in my own way, slowly and with honesty. I did this without questioning my progress and trusted that what I was doing was correct.

My Guided Meditation is all about personal growth and progression, and the key to success in life is truly in your hands. Take the time to use each meditation uniquely, finding a way to make them your own. Bring in your own images and experiences, centering your mind and progressing at your own pace. There isn't a time limit when it comes to personal growth, and meditating will enforce that fact. As you work through this book, try to enjoy each step and turn meditation into something completely special just for you!

Darcy Patrick

Introduction

My Guided Meditation

Using Meditation as a Therapeutic Tool to Focus
Your Overactive Mind and Find Happiness

I started learning to use guided meditation as a part of my therapy and treatment for depression.

My first introduction was when my therapist taught me how to install a safe place in my mind. This was meant to be a place I could go to in my head when I experienced a trigger, or when I felt I was taking a downwards turn. At first, I really didn't think it would help and it was joke! I mean, what was this hippie trippy bull crap? But at that point I was open to anything and I really wanted to change because depression had such a strong hold on my life: it was stopping me from moving forward, and I was trapped in the past, always looking for outside approval for everything did. I was willing to try anything at that point, and accepted all the guidance I was being given from my therapist Mastora Roshan.

The safe place was a very hard thing for me to grasp, and I was not able to do it right away. We had tried five times to install a safe place with me stopping and breaking down each time, and to say it was a struggle would be an understatement. We ended up installing a tree meditation as my safe place and it turned out that this wasn't hippie trippy bull crap after all. I was actually able to relaxed and my mind was clear, and surprisingly I was able to feel the positive effect of installing the safe place right away. This was just the beginning of my experiences with guided meditation and the start of my fight against depression.

The truth is that meditation has been over analyzed for years and it scared me beyond belief. But once I embraced it and made it one of my main tools to combat depression, amazing things started to happen to me. The way I looked at the world changed, how I was able to take myself out of negative situations and calm myself to see things differently was an eye opening game changer in my life. I was able to easily cope with change which was something I had a very hard time with previously. I was able to carry the calm and happiness I felt during and after a meditation with me throughout my day. This greatly impacted me on a daily basis. Not only did it effect me in the ways I just listed, but I learned to use meditation to heal old traumas in my life and use it as healing therapy.

People think you have to empty your mind and go to some mystical place to gain inner peace! Well, meditation is nothing like that: it is actually focusing your mind's power and not letting it bounce from one thing to another. It is all about treating your thoughts with love and using your overactive mind for something you love to do. You'll eventually learn how to travel to places in your mind, getting lost in the moment and learning that your thoughts can be controlled and redirected in ways you never imagined.

This book is going to guide you through learning how to use guided meditation and mindfulness. You will learn how to create your own meditations. These meditations will be special to you and you alone. You will learn to bring all five senses into your meditations, and in doing so it will heighten your experiences and make them even more personal. You will also learn to create your own safe place just for you and you alone. You will learn to use meditation as a personal therapy. When you meditate, everything and anything is in your grasp. Your imagination and the power of your mind will have no restrictions.

What Guided Meditation has Done for Me

Guided meditation, to me, is a wonderful way to deal with the outside world. When I say this I mean what the outside world brings to my life. This means stress from work, stress from family, stress from finances, worry, anxiety, guilt (I hope I didn't miss anything!) but being able to take myself out of this crazy world and into a place that is calm and peaceful is a huge thing. I never thought that it would be such a major part of my life when I start, but my days don't seem right without starting off with a peaceful meditation.

Just taking the time to myself and starting the day calm and relaxed is a simple thing. Starting with a blank slate and an open mind makes the normal stresses in life seem not so big or impossible to deal with. When my mind is clear and calm my thought patterns are healthy, and I am able to find solutions to problems instead of getting overwhelmed and slipping into a downwards turn in my mental state. Calm and level thinking is a major tool in actually living a happy life, loving who you are and remembering that nothing in life is urgent or life threatening. When stresses come up – and they always do – I take the time to calm myself by meditating for five minutes and I come out with a different outlook and a better frame of mind. Whatever was on my mind and stressing me out just doesn't have the same power over me that it did before I meditated.

Being calm and relaxed allows me to not act on emotion or react in an emotional way to situations when they occur. Because of practicing meditation, I have learned to feel the emotion; whether good, bad, or ugly, it doesn't matter. I feel the emotion, and I let the moment pass without acting on it. Feeling emotion is part of being human and we are all human, we are all the same inside. Like it or not we are all in this together, and not one of us is above the other; when it comes to mental health and being happy it is a level playing field. Learning how to meditate has helped me control my emotions and my moods, find happiness in the little things on a daily basis, and carry that happiness throughout my day.

I alone control my moods and being in a calm place allows me to use the tools I was taught to use in therapy and change my negative thought patterns. Guided meditation is the key to using my tools and a major part of starting and maintaining a good day filled with happiness and positive thinking. This is so very important because starting your day in a good frame of mind, being relaxed and centered is what guided meditation is all about. I found that being able to take the time to myself and learning to be patient in practicing meditation gave me the strength and the patience to use my tools in the correct way. Guided meditation has been my key to living a healthy and more fulfilled life.

One of the hardest struggles I had to overcome was actually learning to relax and allowing myself the pleasure of learning this state of mind. The very first thing we will do together is just that – learn to relax.

Learning to Relax

Learning to relax and calm yourself to start a meditation is no easy task. I still fight to calm my mind and push the outside world away, as it is not easy to just turn off. But my secret is that I don't turn off, I just redirect my overactive thoughts towards what I am trying accomplish.

I feel that a lot of people who struggle with anxiety and depression are highly intelligent people who have such powerful minds that they are always focused on something internally while going about their everyday lives. While they are at work, they are thinking about what they have to do when they get home; when they're home, they are thinking about what they have to do at work!

Other times it's thinking about family issues and other things that might happen, or (even worse) they are stuck thinking about the past. I find it no mystery that almost everyone who has this type of overactive mind struggles with depression, anxiety and other mental health issues. When you give these people an outlet in their lives you will find they excel at whatever it is they are doing.

It can be exercise, running, walking, or playing a sport, their forward thinking explodes and they get right into whatever they are doing and can apply the same energy to those activities that they do when they are worrying or when they are stuck in the past thinking about the things that happened to them. It can be too easy to allow past traumas to control their futures and limit their growth as a person.

If you give these overactive-minded people an art form (painting, music, dance, theatre, writing etc.) they will get lost in the moment and they will truly be free. They can become some of the best musicians, painters, dancers, and artists, creating breathtaking works of art and reaching levels in each art form that would blow your mind.

Learning to relax is all about taking control of that overactive, powerful mind, putting it to good use for yourself instead of wasting it on worry and thinking about the past.

The first thing I do when I am relaxing before I meditate is find a peaceful place. That can be anywhere you'd like, such as a park bench, in your bedroom, your living room floor, your sofa – it really can be anywhere you feel at peace. I have meditated sitting on a chair in the middle of a busy downtown street in front of my favorite coffee shop. Anywhere you feel comfortable is the right place to be.

Making sure you are 100% comfortable in the position you are sitting is very important as well. Sometimes I am sitting cross legged in front of my pond and sometimes I am just sitting straight up in a chair, feet on the floor and hands on my knees. However you choose to sit, the main thing is that you feel comfortable in order to relax and calm yourself. If are not comfortable you will never just relax because your mind will be focused on how you need to change the position you are sitting in. If you cannot get comfortable in body then the mind will be distracted and you will never relax.

Once you are comfortable start by breathing deeply with a long inhale through your nose, making sure you feel your chest lift. Feel the breath right to the end of the inhale. Once you are full of air let the air out, and exhale through your mouth. Direct your full attention to your breathing, making sure you are 100% just paying attention to your chest rising and then falling on the exhale. Just paying attention to this and this alone will relax you and take your mind off the outside world and all of its nonsense. When you do this, you are learning to control and focus your overactive, highly intelligent brain.

Just breathing deep and paying attention to your breathing is something we hardly ever do throughout the day and breathing is what gives us life. It is also a dead giveaway for when stress hits us. Your breathing can speed up, become shallow, have you gasping for air, or even make you hold your breath and can cause more stress to what you are feeling already. It's such a simple thing to pay attention to our breathing, but it is very effective.

Take deep slow breaths, and feel your lungs expand and contract. Just breath and think of nothing but that and that alone. Next, once you are totally relaxed and calm, let your mind go and It will wander in different directions. Let it go for a bit but then bring it back by concentrating on your breathing once again. Do this over and over again until you become fully aware of your mind and how it is wanting to go to different places. Let your mind bounce around and then relax it. Bringing it back by concentrating on your breathing is practicing control over your thoughts and is a form of meditation in itself. I will just sit and control my breathing and my mind before every meditation session and that can be 10 minutes or 5 minutes or even 2 minutes if you want.

Breathing Exercises/ Meditation

This breathing exercise is a very calming and a fun thing to practice. It is actually the first meditation we are going to do together in this book. You may have to practice it a lot before you even bring in an image or any senses, so don't get discouraged. Breathing is the building block to guided meditation and must be practiced over and over again. The good news is that it's good for you and you can do it anywhere you'd like, because breathing is what we do to live and just paying attention to it is natural and healthy. Learning to let go of your thoughts is no easy task but learning to bring your mind back from these thoughts is essential. I will practice breathing throughout my day, while I am sitting enjoying my morning coffee, playing with my son, watching a tv show – you name it – breathing deep and paying attention to your breathing is never a bad thing.

Breathing Exercise 1

When I am relaxing I like to do this simple exercise: I will breath deeply, paying attention to my long inhale and exhale, and then I will then let my mind wander off to a particular subject or a thought. I will only allow this one thing in my mind and I will then bring my attention back to my breathing. I will count in my head as I breath in for the whole inhale, counting up from one to five. On the exhale, I will only pay attention to the breath being pushed out. I will repeat 4 or 5 times, then I will relax and let my mind wander again. I will bring myself back from where my mind wandered to by counting to five again on my inhale, and again only concentrating on pushing the air out on the exhale. I will practice this exercise throughout the day, while having a coffee, on lunch break, while on a walk or just sitting by my pond. I will take time out of the day to treat myself to this exercise.

When a stressful situation arises at work I will close my office door and I will practice this exercise, letting the stress and the situation disappear by distracting my mind, focusing on just my breathing. If you are feeling anxious and your body is reacting and showing signs of being overwhelmed, (such as hands shaking, short breaths, heart pounding in your chest) do the breathing exercise. Concentrate on the long inhale. Count to five, then exhale, concentrating on your breath leaving your body, letting your mind go. Learn to control your breathing and your mind at the same time. Once you can do this then using you mind power for a guided meditation is just a step away.

Do this exercise now before reading on and take your time with it. Do not feel rushed, as there is no urgency, no time line for you to follow. Just take your time and learn to bring your mind back to focusing on your inhales and exhales. Breathe and repeat. Allow yourself to reach a calm state. Practice and practice; this is an enjoyable and natural thing to do.

Breathing Exercise 2

Another breathing exercise I love to do and is also the start to using guided meditation is an exercise I like to call "playing with dandelions". This exercise is very simple as it is much like the first exercise we learned to do. You first find a nice comfortable place you feel calm and safe. You then start by taking in that first deep breath and counting to five as you breathe, making sure your breath is deep, paying attention to the full exhale as you breathe out.

Do this over and over again. Then I want you to stop counting to 5, but keep the inhale time the same length - do not change it. Now picture yourself just sitting in a green field... the sky is blue and the sun is shining on you, it's a warm day but not hot, it's just right. You look to your right side, then to your left and there are thousands of dead dandelions all around you. You reach out with your right hand and pull one out of the ground. You pay attention to the air filling your lungs as you inhale. Now on the exhale you make an "O" with your lips and you gently blow, sending the seeds flying from the top of the dandelion.

You drop the dandelion stem, you breath in deep once again, and as you do you watch the seeds float away out of sight. On your exhale you continue to watch those seeds float and dance until you can no longer see them. Now with your left hand pick up another dandelion and repeat the process. Pick as many dandelions as you'd like, stay in this moment for as long as you wish. Picture the green field, the sun, the clouds, see everything as it is, as if you are actually there. Believe it or not, but you are now practicing your first guided meditation.

Just focusing that overactive mind and slowly learning to put it to good use is what this exercise is all about! The more you practice the easier it gets. Do these breathing exercises everyday and take the time out of your day to treat yourself with love and kindness, learn to focus that highly functioning brain and wonderful imagination. Use it for yourself because you are the most important person in your life.

Learning to relax and practicing your breathing is such a wonderful thing to do, learning to treat yourself to the experience of being alive is a gift unto itself. Learning to control your overactive mind goes hand in hand with this and being able to bring both experiences together is such an important thing. Think of these two breathing exercises as pleasurable experiences, grow accustomed to doing them each day and eventually you will start looking forward to practicing them. The peace you will find by doing so will leave you feeling strong and happy! And it leads us to our next step in meditating, which is mindfulness.

Mindfulness Introduction

Mindfulness was taught to me in therapy as way to slow my life down, and to learn to relax and enjoy life. At that time in my life I had a very hard time doing anything for myself without feeling guilty or selfish. Even the smallest act of kindness I would show myself felt unnatural and strange.

My behaviors were backwards and needed to be changed, so my therapist introduced me to mindfulness. We started with a simple act of going to a coffee shop before work to just sit and drink my coffee, and do nothing but enjoy some time alone to myself. It was so hard for me to do this. My thoughts were, "I could be at work right now getting things done before the store opened", or "I could be using this time to catch up on all these guitar repairs". So as I sat there and had these thoughts running through my mind, I did something that I like to do and I wrote. I countered my negative thoughts and I wrote them down.

I could be at work right now getting things done before the store opened.// Why should I do that? I don't get paid for coming in early.

I could catch up on all these repairs.// Why should I take my time before work and use it for something other than what I would like to do? I deserve to be happy, I deserve to do things I love. Work is not my life!

I started to use this time before work to actually enjoy doing something for myself, and who knew that what I enjoyed the most was actually writing! So now I was actually in a hurry to get to the coffee shop so that I could sit and write. I ended up writing eighty percent of "Why I Run" in that coffee shop! And I still can be found there almost every morning before work, just sitting and doing something I love. It was not an easy task at first but over time it became natural. Just like everything in life, we can accomplish great things with practice (and more practice!) and before long the unnatural becomes natural.

Learning to slow down my life and take time for myself was a huge lesson and the power of mindfulness was a big surprise to me. I learned so much about who I am by actually treating myself with love and giving myself the gift of self love. This became a cornerstone to my recovery.

Practicing Mindfulness

This homework assignment was given to me by my therapist, as another way to practice mindfulness. I needed to learn how to slow down and enjoy life, which, when you are suffering from depression, is almost an impossible task. I was in such a deep depression that even doing the smallest thing for myself left me with feelings of guilt. Feeling happiness was totally out of reach, and I often felt that caring for myself was a selfish act. Mindfulness was the first step on overcoming these feelings and learning to feel happiness. It was the gateway to meditation, to feeling good, practicing living in the moment and feeling comfortable with allowing my mind to focus in on details that I never saw before. Getting lost in the details and learning to feel things I had never experienced before was an eye opener. Below is the mindfulness homework I was given. It changed my way of thinking, and I learned that slowing down and loving each moment and the small things in life is where happiness actually lives.

My homework assignment was to eat an orange every morning. I was to take an orange and sit at my kitchen table and place a napkin in front me. Next I was to pick up the orange and roll it around in my hand, noticing everything about the orange. How did it feel? Was it soft or hard, lumpy or bumpy? I was supposed to feel its skin, give the orange a little squeeze. I was to then look at the orange and notice what the skin looked like, focusing on the texture of the skin, all the little imperfections which made each orange perfect unto itself. Notice the different colours of each orange.

How it was yellow in some places and light orange in other places, and dark orange as well. I was able to take notice that each orange was unique, but still just an orange even though nothing about it was perfect.

Then I was to peel this orange, and as I did I watched and paid attention to everything that was about to happen. The sound of the skin as it came off the orange, how I had to break through the skin with my thumb nail. How I would carefully place the peel on the napkin. What was happening to the fruit as I peeled off the skin and the juices were squirting out, covering my hands. I would suck the juices off my thumb and fingers and get a taste for what was going to come next. Just a little tease for what the orange is going to taste like.

Once the orange was peeled I would then break off pieces of the orange and eat it slowly. With each bite, I was to take in all the flavors, notice how each bite of the orange was always different and unique, and in doing so once again I was reminded that nothing is perfect. Even this orange I was eating was not technically perfect but perfect because of its different tastes and textures. When I was finished I took great care to clean up the orange peels and throw them in the garbage.

As hard as this exercise was for me to do at first, over time I actually started to enjoy peeling the orange. I looked forward to eating my orange every morning. I started to pack one in my lunch everyday so when I was at work I could take the time for myself and eat an orange while practicing mindfulness.

This exercise helped me in so many ways. I noticed that every orange was different and that was okay, that being different didn't mean that the orange wasn't an orange but that each one was special. Acknowledging this made me see that life is never perfect, and if I could see that in the orange and still enjoy it, then maybe I could see that in life as well.

Maybe with practice I could change my way of thinking, how I see the world. If doing a simple act like peeling that orange could make such a difference in my life then seeing things in a different light might not be so impossible after all. Maybe I could learn to find happiness in the details that I was not allowing myself to feel before.

Mindfulness slowly became a huge part of my life and I started working it into everything I did. When I was at work repairing guitars, unpacking and counting items, while I was doing the shipping and receiving – the whole time I was working on my mindfulness exercises. Mindfulness has become a part of my everyday health and well-being.

Learning to enjoy the things we do in life has become a lost art, and in this world of fast paced life we get lost in the wrong things and forget what life is all about. We allow outside stress to dictate our happiness and lose sight of the important things in life. We get consumed by accruing material possessions, and we place worth on things that do not matter or have any real worth at all.

Practicing mindfulness brings us back to the simple things in life and allows us to enjoy time to ourselves. Paying attention to all the beauty around us is a gift that can't be bought and the value it has is priceless.

I would like share a mindfulness exercise that I often do when I go for a walk.

Going For a Walk

I like to practice this mindfulness exercise with my son. Dylan loves to get slurpies from our local 7-Eleven in the summer, but he never wants to walk there, despite us living close by. He always wants to go in the car. I make him walk with me because it is good exercise, and as we walk I like to pull different leaves off the trees or bushes as we pass by them.

I hand the leaf to him and ask him to tell me what each leaf feels like: the top of it, then the bottom. He describes it in his own words to me. Then I take the leaf and do the same. I hand it back to him and ask him to count the number of veins in the leaf. Then after he is done, I tell him not to tell me the number and then I count, we then compare the numbers and see if they match. As we walk I pull another leaf off another bush that is completely different from the one we just look at. We then repeat the exercise and compare the differences between the first leaf and the second.

Before we know it we are already at 7-Eleven and the time that we spent walking flew by, creating an experience that was burned into our minds. The impact of this simple mindfulness exercise was felt almost right away. As we walked home Dylan pulled off a leaf from a tree and said, "Hey Dad, look at this leaf! Isn't it cool?" and we would continue to look at leaves on our journey back to the house.

The next day my niece was over for a swim and of course she and Dylan wanted to get slurpies. Instead of driving I made them walk with me again, and as we walked Dylan pulled a leaf off a tree and passed it to his cousin, saying, "Ashley, tell me about the leaf". As we walked we took turns looking at the leaf and on the way home Ashley picked her own leaf from a bush and started to look at it on her own.

I love this exercise. It is one of my favourite mindfulness techniques because every leaf is so different, and there are so many things about each leaf you can notice. And time just passes by as you walk, clear your head and enjoy the moment. The kids never even complained once about how far we walked to get to the 7-Eleven and on the way back we took a longer way home and there was not even one complaint as they were lost in the moment of walking with me, practicing mindfulness without even knowing it. It made time go by fast and easy and it was an enjoyable experience.

Being mindful of our surroundings, our moods and feelings, and taking the time to use our mind power to enjoy simple pleasures is what life is all about. Our minds are not meant to dwell on the past or think about what might or could happen to us in the future. We are not meant to think about things that we have to do or things that must happen. But our minds are meant to enjoy everything around us and learn to love each moment that we are in. Being mindful is simply enjoying life, focusing that overactive mind and being lost in the moment. Purely enjoying life as it happens. The power that you gain by being truly present in your life and being mindful of everything that is happening and both in your mind, body and soul is a superpower and the key to living a happy life.

Our First Guided Meditation

In this meditation I took the peeling the orange exercise and expanded upon it in a major way. The instructions for this are very easy, and will be the same for every meditation we do.

Sit somewhere comfortable and relax, close your eyes and breathe deeply in through your nose and out through your mouth like we did earlier during the relaxation exercises. You can even go to that green field if you'd like and blow the dandelion heads into the air again. Just as long as you reach that state of relaxation, you are ready to continue.

Once you are completely relaxed, take your time and read through the guided meditation below. There will be (*bracketed*) parts where you will be given steps to fully enjoy this experience and truly go there in mind, body and soul. When you reach a bracketed spot you are to close your eyes and picture what you have just read.

As you read, the images that are described will be put into your head, but you will have your own way of seeing each image. That is where your over-active mind will thrive and do amazing things. You will only be limited by your own imagination.

Take your time to fully enjoy the first guided meditation and get lost in the moment.

The Orange

This morning my mind was racing, worries and stress soon crept in, feelings of being trapped and that nothing in my life will ever change were playing on my mind. I acknowledged my feelings and what was happening to me. I began to slow my thoughts down by closing my eyes and taking deep breaths and only paying attention to my breathing.

As I sat cross legged on my blue yoga mat, I just breathed deep and slow. I closed my eyes and truly relaxed, only paying attention to my breathing.

(Take the time now to enjoy your breathing. In through your nose and out through your mouth.)

Once completely relaxed, picture yourself driving a red Ferrari (*Choose any car you dream of driving*) through the rolling hills of an orange plantation in Florida. You come across a huge plantation that is filled with orange trees, large old healthy vibrant trees stretching as far as my eyes could see. These trees are filled with ripe, brightly coloured oranges. The sight is mind blowing: the green trees with oranges highlighting the green back ground. You pull over the car to the side of the road, just on the gravel shoulder. You get out of your car and stand there with amazement at the beauty before you.

(Close your eyes now and picture this image, driving up to the plantation and seeing this wonderful sight, getting out of your car and experiencing everything as if you are there.)

Rows and rows full of orange trees stretch so far that you cannot see the end of any row. You walked across the street and stand at the edge of the plantation; a gentle warm breeze blows by. The smell of fresh oranges ignited your senses (*Feel the breeze and imagine the smell*). You walked into the plantation and say to yourself "I am going to eat one of these oranges". You bend down and take your shoes and socks off and leave them at the edge of the road where the freshly groomed grass leading to the plantation starts. As you walk forward you let the grass massage your feet with every step you take.

(Take the time now to walk in that grass, feel it, experience each step.)

You approached a fabulous mature tree, its limbs are huge and it has a wonderful shape to it. All its limbs and branches create an intricate umbrella above you, shading you from the hot sun. You looked up and see the perfect orange, round, vibrant, filled with juice, ripe and ready to burst at any moment. You reach up and have to stretch every muscle in your body to reach this orange and pluck it from its branch. The orange is the size of a softball and it is heavy, ripe and ready to eat.

(Picture this orange and imagine its weight as you hold it in your hand, try to see everything about the orange you can in detail.)

You walked away from the tree with your prize, and you see an old fashioned hand pump on your right side. You take the heavy, swollen orange over to the rusty handled pump and begin to pump, up and down on it. Before you know it the pump is bursting out fresh, clean, cold water from the depths of its well.

(Picture the cold water rushing out and the feeling you have as the water hits your hands.)

You hold the orange in your left hand and pump the water over it with your right, and you wash the orange clean.

Through the corner of your eye off to the left you see a small round wooden table, it is only about 1 foot tall and about 12 inches around and there is a wood bowl sitting on. The bowl is about halfway filled with orange peels. There is a white cotton towel there as well, for drying your hands off after eating your orange. You walk over and sit cross legged beside this table.

(Picture the table now – what does it look like? Try to see the detail as you walk over to it.)

You take a bite out of the bottom of the orange. You pull the center of the peel out with your teeth. The juice covers your face and the taste is out of this world, like no orange you have ever tasted. Tangy and sweet at the same time. So fresh your taste buds are put into overdrive.

(Truly imagine what this orange tastes like, take your time and do not rush this experience.)

You place the center of the orange peel in the wooden bowl and you begin to peel the orange with care. You dig your thumb in between the peel and the flesh of the orange and pull it back.

(Imagine what is happening now. What sounds do you here as the peel is pull away from the flesh of the fruit?)

With each piece of orange peel you remove, your hands are drenched with its juices. You suck the juices off your thumb as you place the peels in the bowl.

(Now peel this orange and try to experience everything you can: sight, sound, smell, taste; leave nothing out.)

Once the orange is peeled you break it in half and place one half on the table. The other half you will carefully peel each layer off and eat it. The pieces of the orange melt in your mouth, each one sweeter than the one before *(Imagine the taste explosion with every bite you take, how each peace is an experience)*. You finish the first half and move on to the second.

The second half you just pick up and take a big bite of, and the orange explodes in your mouth, all over your face. The juices are running down your face and neck but you don't care, you just take another bite and enjoy this moment fully, the tastes, sights, the smells and sounds of this wonderful experience. After you finished, you take the white towel and clean yourself up.

You walk over to the hand pump and you wash your face off with the cold well water. You slowly walk over to where your shoes and socks are at the edge of the road, where the gravel meets the grass. You slowly put your socks and shoes on. Before you leave you take one more long look at this wonderful orange plantation.

(*Imagine what this place looks like, try to burn it into your mind and see, hear, smell everything.*) You get back in your red Ferrari and drive away.

Now slowly breath deep like we did when we started this meditation. In through your nose and out through your mouth, take you time and when you are ready, open your eyes. Notice how calm, happy, and free from stress you are, how strong and proud you feel. Let the memories of visiting this orange plantation stay with you and allow yourself to feel this happy feeling throughout your day.

The power of our minds blows me away at times. The times that we can spend stewing, worrying, building anxiety and sinking deep into a depressed state are wasting this mind power and not actually seeing just how smart we are. But then to create such a wonderful and vibrant place in our minds truly shows the power that each and every one of us has. It is truly amazing how once we focus our minds, what wonderful things we are capable of doing.

I strongly feel that people like me who are blessed with an overactive mind just need a way to put that power to good use, learn how to focus and draw on the good and not the bad in life. I say blessed with an over active mind now, but before I thought I was cursed and only saw the bad in life. To do a meditation like we just did is proof that our minds are capable of doing so many things in life. Just learning to focus (and most of all practice,practice, practice!) is the most important thing we can do when learning new skills for truly being happy.

Attention to Detail

How to Start Building Your Own Meditations

When I start to build a guided meditation, I come up with a place in my mind I would like to go to. I will use a memory I have, a very good experience or something that was truly wonderful that happened to me. Maybe even a wild fantasy, it doesn't matter how outrageous it is or if it is completely impossible, nothing is out of bounds. The greatest thing is we all have these images, these places, these fantasies, we just have to learn to feel free to go there. Being free in our thoughts and practicing mindfulness and bringing in all that detail and truly using it to enhance our meditations is what we need to do.

Once you have your place, try to bring all your senses into play. What you see, hear, smell, touched, even tasted. These things will help you get to that place. You are in charge of your life and your meditations, throw caution to the wind and have fun, make these magic moments your own. That's what makes it so powerful. The power to just transport yourself to anytime, anyplace, doing anything you wish to is in your hands!

Below is how I approach using each sense when I build a meditation. Practicing mindfulness is very simple and natural, let yourself be free and unlock your mind.

Combining writing with our meditations is a powerful tool. I like to write out examples of each sense, as this helps me truly go to these places. I not only focus my mind but also by physically writing it on paper I truly burn these images and details into my mind and in doing so I truly experience the meditation I am creating.

Sight:

I think of wonderful colours created by a sunrise, the mixing of the sun with the clouds making unique shades of red, blue, pink, and purple. When I am on a morning run I will look to the sky to see just what is happening, and I make a mental note to remember what I saw. I write it down when I'm home so I can go back and read it.

When walking to work I take notice of people's front yards and get a good look at what is growing. Big wonderful bushes with different shades of green, how thick they are, how their leaves intertwine to make a solid bush. Blooming flowers just exploding before my eyes. How unique each flower is, how their colours are so vibrant and special. I save all these sights in my mind and in doing so I am practicing mindfulness.

I remember trips with my family when I was a child and new trips with my own family now. Waterfalls, nature paths, lakes, streams, fast flowing rivers. Sight is the building block and the most powerful thing when meditating for me. I build on top of an image and bring in the other senses as I go. I transport myself to that time or place. I will also make up a place that doesn't even exist by mixing all my experiences together to make a wonderful place just for me. I bring in all the imagery I have in mind and I melt it into the places I create. If you can imagine it, then you can make it happen in your head.

There are no rules here, no restrictions to what you can picture in your mind; you can go anywhere you'd like at any time. Do anything you wish, total freedom of mind and body is what we are after. Creating a place just for you is a wonderful personal accomplishment.

Sound:

Sound is soothing and relaxing, bringing sound into a meditation can transport you to where you would like to be pretty fast. I sometimes use the sound of my backyard waterfall to wash away my problems after a hard day, or start the day with a clean slate after the waterfall washes everything away. Even in the dead of winter I will use the sound of my backyard waterfall to transport me to a summer day, sitting beside my pond. Using the sound of my pond and allowing it to bring me back to that place in time is truly an experience.

There are so many ways to use natural sounds in the world to bring your meditation to life.

For example:

- A calm breeze blowing through trees leaves creating a rustling sound
- The sound of waves whooshing onto the shore of a beach
- Birds chirping in the morning
- Toads calling to their friends

Sound is so powerful, and repetitive sounds work as well for meditations. They distract you from the outside world and at the same time create an almost hypnotizing feeling.

Sometimes just hearing certain sounds can trigger memories. The sound of a dog catching a Frisbee, for example, brings me to a special time in my life where I was playing Frisbee with my dog at the park down the street from my house. Just thinking about the sound now brings back an image I haven't seen in five years.

Use sound to bring you to the places you are picturing: if you are walking in the woods, try to hear the birds chirping, sticks snapping under your feet, a breeze blowing the leaves in the trees. Maybe you even hear the sound of a creek gently running in the background. Capture the sounds you may hear in those woods. Whatever the moment you are wishing to create, adding whatever sounds go along with it is very simple but very effective. Sound will bring you there.

How many times have you heard a song on the radio and it has brought back memories of a certain time? Being with friends, sitting quietly and listening to music is a wonderful experience. Music can bring back memories of a party you were at, the people you were with and the good times that you had.

Music can bring back memories of so many things. When I hear "Have I Told You Lately That I Love You" I am brought back to my wedding day as that song was my first dance with my wife. When I hear "Twist and Shout" I remember playing in my first band with my friends and it was the only song we knew, so we played it over and over again! When I hear the "The Ballad of John and Yoko" I remember learning how to play that song on my bass guitar, as it was the first song I learned to play by ear. I remember the bass I was playing, my parents rec room, the wallpaper, the album as I had to keep lifting the needle and playing it over as I learned each note. I also remember how proud I was when I could finally play through the song without stopping.

We have so many memories connected to sound and music and the wonderful thing is that each and every one of us have different memories that we can draw on.

Sound is powerful and is part of our tool box when creating a guided meditation.

Smell:

Smell can transport you to any place in a matter of seconds; even just a faint smell of something can trigger memories in our mind. Smell is powerful and using it is very important. There are certain smells that just ignite our brains, bring goosebumps to our skin and make our hair stand up on end. Scents can even trigger memories of people who have passed away. Grandparents can be an example of this. The smell of your grandmother's perfume will bring back great memories of her. Maybe the smell of a pipe being smoked would trigger a mental picture of your grandfather sitting with that pipe after dinner. The smell of cookies baking, soup cooking, bread baking may bring back vivid memories.

Coffee percolating always makes me feel calm and relaxed. So many smells to use and tie in with what you are seeing and hearing when it comes to writing your meditations. Walking in the woods brings the smell of wet damp wood. Walking past a garden brings smells of roses, lavender, honeysuckles blooming. These smells bring images and even emotions to life in our bodies.

If you're sitting on the beach in your mind, maybe imagine the smell of wet sand, maybe the faint smell of seaweed drying in the sun. The sunscreen you just applied to your skin. A campfire burning as you sit with your family or friends roasting marshmallows. On a fishing trip sitting on a bank of a river, think of the smells you might come into contact with. Write down various scents, building a list of what smells you love.

Sometimes it's easy and sometimes it's hard to find a smell for a specific location because sometimes places just don't have a scent and that's okay. If there is no smell, no problem, just leave it out and keep building. Again this is your meditation and you can make it anyway you want it to be.

Touch/Feeling:

Touch/feeling a big sense to draw on when crafting your guided meditations. Touching something with your hands, feeling the textures like soft, hard, slippery, wet, prickly, slimy, waxy, sticky, sharp, dull, the list goes on and on. I like to practice enjoying the sense of touch when I am running or on a walk. I will pull a leaf from a tree and rub it between my fingers and thumb, feeling its texture and the veins that run through the leaf. Is it soft or waxy, fuzzy on the underside or slick and slippery, is it tough? Can you easily rip it? Or is it hard to rip? Remember all these different textures and use them. This ties back into the mindfulness exercise of eating an orange. Running your hand over its skin and feeling the bumps and lumps before ripping it open to eat.

Touch is an exciting sense because it is what your body is feeling when it comes in contact with other things. The sun warming your skin on a hot summer day while you are walking on a beach. The breeze cooling you off when you get out of a stream you were swimming in. The rain falling on you as you walk through a jungle you created. The feeling you get when the hair stands up on the back of your neck, after you hear a song on the radio you like, or if you think of something scary. The warmth of the water you are in when sitting in a hot spring. The heat from the camp fire you are sitting in front of. The cold shock you get when diving into a cold lake up north at a cottage. Touch/feeling is a strong sense and they capture the moment you are in.

The impact of your surroundings on your physical being can effect you while you are meditating. The ability to actually feel the environments you are in is a power that we all have and you can bring it to life! Our bodies feel everything and our minds and souls are directly connected. Once you start learning to bring the sense of touch/ feeling to life while you meditate you are really making use of your overactive and powerful mind.

Taste:

Last but not least is the sense of taste. The explosive taste of that orange, a fresh ripe peach, a sour apple, grapes freshly picked from the vine - just thinking about it makes my mouth water. Remembering eating the best dinner you have ever had, biting into it and feeling the textures of the food—with each bite and movement of your mouth new flavors are released. Eating ice cream and having it melt in your mouth. So many possibilities are there, you just have to draw on them. Below is an example of a great meal I had. In this example I allow the tastes to trigger so many memories of that night, of the great meal I had, the good company that I was with. Enjoy this short meditation, as I write about this dinner and in doing so I burn the memory into my mind and bring it to life at the same time.

When I was in Montana on business, I was treated to many good meals. One stands out the most, and that was a bison steak I ordered at a restaurant. The bison was local and aged to perfection.

I like my meat rare and I had never had bison before so I was very excited when it came to the table. The meal consisted of fresh vegetables cooked perfectly with grill markings seared onto them. Green broccoli, red and green peppers and my favorite of all vegetables, asparagus, dressed in balsamic vinegar. (*Picture these vegetables on the plate now, smell them cooked in the vinegar*). But the bison was the greatest thing on the plate. There was just the right amount of red for me. It was about the size of a softball and you could see the different seasonings and fresh ground pepper on the top. There were grill marks on both sides, black and freshly seared. (*See this steak, on the plate, and imagine what it looks like, what it smells like, see the different textures of this piece of meat, the different colours of the vegetables all mixed together on the plate – bring it to life*).

I sliced into the steak with my sharp knife, holding it by the strong wooden handle. The knife sliced through the meat like butter. The meat was so tender and had zero fat, no grizzle, a perfect cut just for me. (*Picture cutting into this steak, make it as real as you can*) I put the small slice I had cut in my mouth and the taste was out of this world! The meat just melted in my mouth, I barely had to chew. I could taste just a little bit of seared meat followed by a little bit of ground pepper they used for flavor.

I followed it up with a bite of the grilled asparagus, then washed it all down with a swig of beer that was brewed locally. A dark amber ale with a very wheat flavored aftertaste and a honey overtone. (*Taste this now, take the time to imagine all the tastes, bring it to life like you are there*)

I slowly then cut off another piece from my steak and took my time to enjoy each bite. As I eat I mix each bite with tastes from each vegetable on my plate. I made sure that I enjoyed each bite and enjoyed each flavour. As I write this my mouth is actually watering.

This meal was outstanding and is burnt into my mind mainly because of the tastes. Those tastes alone transport me back to that dinner and the friends who were there, the laughter, the conversations and even the music that was playing. The whole experience just comes back to life as I picture myself in the restaurant sitting and enjoying that meal.

The power of our senses is incredible. Use as many of the senses as you can and it will enrich and make your meditations so much more enjoy able. I suggest that before you even start the next section you just sit and make a list of all the things you can experience under each sense. Go into great detail and try make a long list for each one. Don't be afraid to list any experiences you have had because every one is special and unique to you and may hold their own special meanings. This is practicing mindfulness and this is a building block in our goal of building a guided meditation.

Starting A Guided Meditation

In this book I will share with you my guided meditations. These are my most private places I have gone to in my mind, and my thoughts before and after I am finished each one. Please just use these meditations as guidelines and ideas for your own meditations. These are not meant to be strict outlines but they are meant to inspire you and help you reach your goal of creating your own meditations.

You can use my meditations in different ways.

First, you can read what I have written and slowly go there as you read and transport yourself to each place, bring in your senses, using them along with what I have written. But only use my meditations as frame work for your own experiences. Highlight them with your own mind, making it look and sound and feel the way you want it to. Draw on the tools we just learned about and transport yourself there. Make sure you stop along the way and close your eyes and truly go to these places as there will be *(bracketed)* sections with instructions throughout the written meditations.

Second, you can just read through my stories and get an idea of where the experience is taking place. Get a feel for what I am trying to create. After you read through them, then go there yourself. Use your senses and create this place yourself. You are only limited by your imagination. Remember that there are no rules so be free with your mind and expand on my examples in any way you wish.

Third, there are specific meditations that I have written for certain situations. These meditations were meant to help me cope with what was happening in my life at that time. The goal would be that you as the reader could see yourself in these meditations and then be able to use the framework to help you in a way that is comfortable for you. That you can make these therapeutic meditations a personal experience and in doing so make them a special place for you! And that is once again where the magic is, the true power of our minds, being put to good use.

Repetition is Key

The key to everything we do in life is repetition, so when working out of this book do not rush through anything. Take the time to make sure you feel good each and every step along the way. Make sure breathing is the first thing you do when starting these meditations. You can just work on one meditation for a long time until you feel comfortable, do the same one everyday for a month or longer if you'd like: it is okay and all part of the experience. The goal is to create a special place just for you with as much detail as possible. The more you practice meditation, the better you will become at applying it.

Don't feel you have to move on because there are ten meditations in this book. There are no prizes for levels achieved and they don't get harder as you read through the book. Each one is just a framework for you to build upon, ideas for you to use and before you know it you will have your own places to go to. Meditation is an exercise of mind, body, and soul. When you are able to focus that extremely creative and powerful mind and use it for your own good, paying attention to every detail and every nuance in a meditation, then you are truly unlocking the power of your mind. You will be able to reach a deep meditative state and truly treat yourself with love.

Throughout life we are faced with completing different tasks. Whether it be at work or play, nothing comes natural right away, it always takes practice and then more practice. As we do things over and over again we naturally learn what works and what does not.

When learning to skate we take our time, because at first just being able to stand in skates on ice is a hard task. I like to think of this as learning to breathe when starting to meditate.

When you were able to stand in skates you wanted to move, and you fell over and over again. There is no simpler way of describing it but you got back up, steadied yourself and over time learned to move forward. You made mental notes, reacted to how your body was moving on the ice, corrected your movements and soon you learned not to fall. The same goes for learning how to keep your breathing calm and learning to bring in your senses. Over time you just skate as you learn how to control your movements.

When you start to bring in imagery, going to these places in your mind will have you pulling yourself up numerous times from falling down. Learning to let your mind wander and then bringing it back, for example. The act of repetition when learning to meditate is actually meditating, you just don't know it because you are learning!

So practice and then practice some more, repeat over and over again until you miss repeating and then take pride in what you have done!

When to Practice Meditation, Relaxation and Mindfulness

I love to start my day with being mindful of how I am feeling, both my emotional state and my physical state. I like to use my tools first thing in the morning. I will wake up earlier then the rest of the house, but if you don't have a family then just wake up earlier then normal. I like to give myself 2 hours in the morning but that is a little excessive, but it is what I love to do. I find that starting my day by using my tools does two things.

It allows me to change my thinking and emotional state if I am feeling off. Then I can start my day calm and open-minded. Whatever was playing on my mind is now gone and I have replaced my emotional state with one I wish to be in. This feels so good to achieve because it builds confidence and shows you just how strong you are when you start off your day by changing your outlook and emotional state to a way you want to be feeling instead. This proves to yourself that moments in time do not have to influence your whole day. If you take the time to sit down and truly be in touch with your mind, body and soul it translates into the rest of your day. You are able to keep that connection and feel so much pride in doing so.

Later on in the day I also like to take a break and check in with myself, typically at lunch time. I like to sit and notice how my day is going. I will reflect and maybe even write about it in my journal. I take the time to meditate and in doing so celebrate just how well my day is going because I am in control and I am able to treat myself with love and kindness. Also, if things are not going that good I love to take the time and remember just how good I felt in the morning. Doing this instills the fact that the next half of my day can change and I do not have to have a bad day. After all, I was able to meditate earlier that day and if I changed my emotional state then I can now change it again!

At the end of the day I like to once again reflect on the day that has passed and also calm myself for a good night's sleep, making sure that anything that is playing on my mind is soon washed way and dealt with in a positive fashion.

Being able to integrate mindfulness and meditation into our everyday lives is a wonderful way to live! Who doesn't like being happy and feeling love? Ending a day and beginning a new one without being stressed is a wonderful feeling. Over time this way of living becomes natural. You will suddenly find yourself feeling good and practicing what you are learning without thinking of it. Just like skating, riding a bike or doing anything you love, meditation will become a natural part of your life.

Using Meditation as a Tool to Help With Stress and Anxiety

I like to use the following meditations when stress and anxiety come into my life. For me some of these stresses come about because of work. Our workplace can be the main factors in our daily health and well-being. Seeing that we spend eighty percent of our day at work we need to find a way to be healthy in our workplaces in mind and body and soul.

If you really think about it, we wake up and see our families or have maybe a maximum of two hours to ourselves before we go to work. When we leave work we come home eat dinner and then go to bed. Then we spend maybe two hours in the evening with our family again or spend time alone. Maybe sleeping or not sleeping because we have so much rolling around in our heads from the events at work that day. We then wake up and start it all over again. The other stressful factors in life other than work could be finances, family crisis, etc. We all have our own things that affect us on a daily basis. Being able to see this and know our reactions is the first and most important step to alleviating stress. Having a way of changing our reactions and our outlook is the next step.

I came up with two very impactful meditations that work best for me when I am at work. When my heart starts to jump and my anxiety goes through the roof, I go to these places to escape and enjoy my time alone, regroup and change my mood. By just taking the time to completely leave my work place in my min,. I am able take control and be happy, calm and able to think in a positive manner/have balanced thoughts.

I carry these meditations with me throughout my day and feel the freedom and joy they bring me even after I have finished the actual meditation. When I am faced with a problem and I can feel the effects of stress and anxiety come over me I am able to be calm, go to the place I created and use that calm and happiness to get me through my day.

The two meditations I am going to share are "Flying in the Clouds" and "The Great Escape".

Flying in the Clouds

Have you ever wanted to just fly away and leave the world behind? Have you ever looked up at the clouds and thought "What would it be like to play in those fluffy masses? How would it feel to be up that high in the air? What do clouds really feel like?" In this meditation, we will do just that: we will push the power of our minds and we will fly to the clouds and play in them, and it will be our own little secret!

Flying in the clouds is a meditation that came to me while I was at work feeling overwhelmed, trapped, and not able to breath. I would walk outside of my work and lean up against the wall. I would breath deeply and look to the sky, and I would see the clouds floating by and think to myself "If only I could be up there." Free from all that is on my mind, free from the stress and the emotions that were overflowing inside me.

I remember saying to myself, why can't I go up to the clouds and play? Why can't this be a place I have to go to when I have to deal with work stress, when I start to feel trapped and overwhelmed? So closed my eyes and I came up with flying in the clouds! Enjoy.

Today is a good day to lose ourselves in the clouds, white puffy clouds. A day where you sneak off outside, out of sight. You have a special power that no one knows about! You are able to fly! But no one can ever find out about this power or you will lose it instantly and never get it back. So when you use it, it has to be a secret!

(Make sure you are somewhere comfortable, breath deep and relax. Imagine walking outside and hiding behind something, and begin this meditation.)

You close your eyes, breath deeply and empty your mind. Think only of your breath, in and out, feeling each breath from the beginning and then out to the end. You become lighter than air and begin to float slowly, raising off the ground, your body becoming weightless and gravity has no effect at all. You float up, up, up into the sky. *(Just breath deep and feel what it must feel like to be weightless.)*

As you float, open your eyes and look down below you (*What do you see? picture it as you rise into the sky*) look up to the sky (*What do you see?*). The world below is not on your mind anymore because it is gone for now. Only flying is on your mind! As you look to the clouds above, you practice your flying skills.

(What you are doing as you fly? You can do anything you would like to you, you are the one flying, there are no physical boundaries when you are flying so feel free to do whatever you'd like, play in the sky as you fly up to the clouds.)

After flying for some time you just move side to side, and you learn to speed up as you bring your hands over your head and slow down as you put them on your waist. You get used to the feeling of the wind passing by and the control you have over your upward motion.

Don't go too fast, you want this flight to last! You want to enjoy your trip to the clouds.

As you get higher and higher you begin to pass through little wisps of clouds, nothing thick, and you reach out and let the soft wisps pass through your hands. Gently tickle them with your fingers as you raise higher and higher.

(Feel the clouds passing through your fingers)

Before you know it, you are surrounded by thick clouds and you speed up and pass through as fast as you can.

(How does the sensation of passing through these thick clouds feel? Use all the detail you can.)

You reach the top of the clouds and you drop down and rest on them. The feeling is amazing. It is like being on a trampoline but softer. You bounce with every step but the surface is forgiving at the same time, and the clouds hold your weight. You will not slip through.

(Take the time to imagine just what standing on these clouds feels like, lose yourself in the moment and take your time!)

You decide to start your adventure! You start by doing running jumps, one foot at a time, pushing yourself forward and gliding in the air before placing your other foot down. You slowly build up speed, and before you know it you are moving at a fast pace and flying ten feet with each footstep you take.

(How do you feel right now? Think about the freedom you have and just let that freedom fill you with joy, there is nothing but you and the clouds)

Ahead, you see a break in the clouds.

You time your steps so when you reach the break in the clouds perfectly, you jump in the air and fly thirty feet to the next cloud.

(What do you see as you are airborne? Look down try to picture everything as you pass over the gap in the clouds.)

You make the jump with ease and land with both feet hitting the ground at the same time. You are once again airborne, flying straight up into the air! You come down and land perfectly. You smile and think to yourself, "That was so much fun!" But now it is time to just jump like you are on a trampoline.

You start jumping straight up into the air and build up height until you are comfortable. Once you are comfortable, start your routine! You are an Olympic athlete!

(Now just relax and picture yourself going through a routine. It can be as dangerous and long as you'd like.)

Imagine you are going for a gold metal! You finish up with some flips and twists and land the perfect landing! You feel proud and it's like nothing you have ever felt before. (*Feel this emotion fully as you are truly free in the clouds!*)

Now it is time to go for a little swim in the clouds: you close your eyes, empty your mind and sink into the clouds just enough for your head to be peeking out above them.

(What does this feel like? Imagine what being surrounded by thick clouds feels like.)

Take a deep breath and fill your lungs with this wonderful, super clean air and start swimming hand over hand, feet kicking and building up some speed, then just glide through the clouds. You are passing through them at a high speed.

(Feel the speed you have built up, how you are cutting through the clouds, you are a superhero!)

The clouds are massaging you as you glide through them. You roll over on to your back and start a nice relaxed back stroke, slowing your speed. Look up at the clear blue sky and wonder what it is like out above you in space.

You then let yourself glide to a stop. Once again, close your eyes, empty your mind and raise above the clouds. You now take a good look around before closing your eyes, emptying your mind and slowly float back down through the clouds.

(See this wonderful sight, take it all in, burn it into your mind!) You will now slowly float back to earth, back through the clouds. (*Feel the clouds as you pass through them on your way back to the ground.*)

Burn the memory of your descent into your mind, and notice how the wind surrounds you and blows you from side to side. Put your hands out at your sides and steady yourself as you glide back down to the ground. (*Feel free to have fun as you travel back to the earth.*)

When you touch down, take the time to breathe deeply and take notice of the relaxed state you are in. Look at your watch; you were only gone for ten minutes! What a trip! You feel free, refreshed, happy, and filled with joy. Another trip to the clouds is complete and your secret is still safe!!

I hope that you enjoyed this mediation and I also hope that that you were able to fill in as much detail as you could in the places I left open for you. Remember that you aren't being graded, there is no right or wrong way to do your meditation, just how good you feel while you are in these different places. The more you practice, the better each experience will become.

This is a fun meditation because you have control over how your body is reacting to flying and playing in the clouds. Control is something that we all like to have in our lives, and when you meditate, you give yourself that control. You go to the places you want to go to in your mind and you experience the things you want to experience. Learning and practicing this leads to your own personal growth and lets you learn to treat yourself with love and kindness. It costs nothing to allow yourself to experience these things through guided meditation. Meditation is a tool you can use any time you wish and every time you use a meditation, you benefit from it.

Flying in the clouds is one of my favorite meditations to carry with me at all times. I have it in the back of my mind all day, every day. I like to think of it like when I was young in grade school and I would be off daydreaming. When I am at work I like to day dream about my trips to the clouds. I like to feel the freedom that I experience when I am in the clouds. I like to close my eyes for a few seconds and be on top of those clouds, remember everything and feeling the emotions that I felt when I was in the meditation.

I will also sneak away after having to deal with a stressful situation, or if I want to clear my head before I deal with a situation that I know will be stressful. I need to have my full attention and emotions in check. I will close my eyes and I will go to the clouds and play, put my life on hold and give myself a fresh perspective as to what really matters and what doesn't. It is very easy to get caught up in the moment and act in a way that we normally would never act. Being able to have this meditation in my back pocket to use is a total bonus! I take pride in having it. Sometimes on a really beautiful day I will look up to the sky and smile as I watch the clouds pass by, knowing that I could be up there too!

The Great Escape

Everyone has dreamed about escaping at one point in their life, being free from all of their strings and responsibilities. I think many people have imagined how good it would be to win the lottery and pay off their debt, not having to go to work anymore. Being able to call work and say "I will never be back again!" is something many people have fantasized about, and telling your boss to shove it is a dream! Just escaping that part of your life altogether would be great for most people, as the vast majority of stress in life stems from unhappiness in the workplace.

Wouldn't it be nice to experience that thrill for just a while? Experience the whole feeling from the beginning to the end. Have a life where you wake up in the morning and it is like you are on vacation! No plans, no urgent things that you feel you have to do! Below is a meditation I like to use to escape every once in a while. Read through it and bring yourself there completely while you read. Then when you are finished, take time to reflect. Make your own ending and remember that you are not limited by anything, your wildest dreams can come true! Escape with me – let's go!

Picture yourself pulling up to the 7-Eleven or convenience store down the street from your house and walking in, waiting in line patiently to buy some cream for your morning coffee. While in line you remember that you have a lottery ticket to check. When you finally get to the till and pay for your cream, you hand the ticket to the cashier and tell her that you have a "winning ticket!" It was a birthday gift from a friend, so it has to be lucky. *(This ticket is the key to your great escape, feel the excitement of this moment.)*

The cashier takes the ticket from your hand and puts it into the scanner like she has done thousands of times before, but this time it is different! The machine plays its prerecorded song and a voice says "Winner, gagnon!" The screen displays "GRAND PRIZE WINNER! Please contact the OLG." The cashiers face goes blank. Nothing like this has ever happened to her and she is dumbfounded, completely speechless. She gives you the ticket back and says "You just won the lottery! 25 million dollars, wow... the great escape begins!"

(Imagine the feeling now! Truly feel the emotion as if you just won 25 million dollars!)

You go outside to your car and use your cell phone to call work. Your boss answers the phone and you tell them "I will not be coming into work today or any other day! I have just won the lottery and I QUIT!" Your heart is racing, so you sit in the car for a moment as you realize that your life has just changed in a major way.

(Take the time here to really just imagine sitting in your car and feeling everything that you would feel if you found out you just won this money! Scream with joy if you like! Let your heart race as you make this meditation as real as you want it to be.)

The next thing is calling the lottery office and telling them you have a winning ticket. *(Imagine calling now, getting the address to the building and saying you will be there in an hour.)* You now pick up your wife or husband, friend, someone you wish to bring with you. Or maybe this is a solo trip and you are doing this on your own.

(Think about this moment and realize that you are free to move forward in any way you wish, this is your escape and you meditation, your fantasy.)

As you drive on the highway to pick up your cheque, your mind is racing thinking about how your life has just changed, your debt will be wiped way and you are now free!

(Let your mind go now - what is the first thing you will do with the money? Give yourself this pleasure now as you have a bit of a drive to get the cheque, make it real and feel the emotion in your body as you truly embrace this moment.)

When you finally get to the office, you park your car and walk through the front door. You push open the large glass double doors like you own the place, confident and happy. You walk over to the front desk and give your name. They welcome you with open arms, so happy to greet the winner of the grand prize. *(Now picture yourself there: what does the place look like?)* They take you into a back office to check your ticket.

(What does the office look like, what do you see, hear, or smell? Do they take your picture with a big cheque? Get lost in the details, be free because this is your great escape. What happens next? Make it as real as you'd like.)

Once you get the cheque you are amazed at the amount of zeros there are in the number.

(Feel the emotion now as if this is truly really happening.)

You walk out of the building and on to the busy street. You follow the directions to the bank to cash the cheque! 25 million, holy smokes. You ask for no limit to be put on your bank card, and the lady at the till smiles and says "Congratulations on the big win!"

As you walk out of the bank, the sky is the limit now, and the first thing you want to do is go away on a trip.

(This is a far as we will go now. You will now close your eyes and you will finish this meditation in any way you want to. This is your time now, take this in any direction you choose. When you are finished your great escape, read below.)

The great escape is such a great meditation because who doesn't want to escape their life at certain times? It is an idea, a place, a state of mind. The thought of complete freedom and nothing stopping you from that escape is a wonderful thought, but the secret to this meditation is that you actually gained this freedom without money. You used the power of your mind to create this adventure and to calm yourself and change your mood.

I used the twenty five million dollar figure because so many people (especially when it comes to work stress) see the only way out as having an endless amount of money to draw on to free themselves fully. But the truth is that when you open your mind to change and you do a meditation like what we just did and go there truly in your mind, you accept it and free yourself from what is on your mind. You are free from worry and stress, you escaped and it didn't cost a thing.

Why waste mind power on things you can't control, on situations that haven't happened yet or may never happen at all? We work ourselves up so badly in our minds at times that we lose sleep and just make the problems bigger, but we can do the great escape instead! It enforces that our minds are capable of doing amazing things.

I have often used both The Great Escape and Flying In The Clouds while at work, before work even starts, so I have the memories, feeling and emotions planted in the back of my mind. So when my mind starts wandering to places it doesn't need to go to or my mood is effected by work stress, I have a solid place and I remember that I control my emotions. While the world is spinning out of control, I am escaping or flying in the clouds.

Practice these meditations and make them your own, add to them, use as much detail as you can and enjoy them!

Physical Movement and Meditation

When we work on bettering ourselves it is not only important to involve our minds but our bodies as well. For example, I do yoga and run.

When I do my yoga routines I will bring myself to a meditative state, leave my body altogether and imagine that I am some place wonderful and exciting. I will start with deep breathing and just concentrate on the poses, letting my mind drift. As I do this I bring in a place I would like to go. I take notice of my thoughts and focus them because they will almost always go towards the things I feel I need to do or things that I might have on my mind from work.

I take that wasted mind power and focus it on something nice. I will go to a mountain top and I will see and smell everything. I will go through my yoga poses as if I am right there, forest in front of me, mountains behind the forest framing it all, beauty all around me. I will go through my routine and as I do I will take a moment between each pose to relax and enjoy where I am, making the detail greater as I spend my time doing the meditation. You can apply this to any physical exercise you are doing.

While on a walk, you can breathe deeply and as you walk you can have a vision in your mind that you can expand upon. You will find that your walk just got a lot more interesting, the walk will not seem so long, the time you spent will not seem so wasted. You will actually get lost in the moment and you can bring things you see on your walk into your meditation.

You will start looking forward to your walks and they will become more enjoyable each time. What once may have seemed like a chore to do now becomes a treat and a place you can't wait to get to!

I find the problem with most people is that they see exercise as boring and feel it is something they have to do to lose weight and get into shape, but their time is being wasted doing the activity. Whatever activity they are doing feels like a chore.

Actually, doing something for one's own enjoyment in these days of work and more work is something that has to be taught to us again. When we were children we couldn't wait to play, we looked forward to it and we enjoyed it fully when the time finally came. Somewhere along the way as we became adults, all of this just disappeared out of our lives. We teach ourselves that adults have to stop playing and enjoying life and have to make money, there's no time anymore for fun and play.

When you learn to meditate while you work out or run or walk, whatever you like to do, time flies by much faster and you feel so free at the end of it.

Meditation mixed with your physical movement can actually help create memories that you can use throughout the day while you are at work or school. In grade school they called this daydreaming and wanted you to stop and concentrate on your work. When I was in grade school and high school I was almost never where I should have been mentally while I was sitting in the class room. I was day dreaming all the time, but that is actually a healthy way of dealing with stress and making the hard things in life not so hard anymore, and believe it or not, daydreaming becomes really enjoyable.

For example, I do my tree meditation almost every day while I run. One day while I was running I went to my tree and pictured foxes playing under my branches in the shade I was providing. I watched them rolling around and nipping at each other playfully and just having a fun time. I used great detail and I burned that memory into my mind. I remember how lost in the moment I actually was, the feelings I experienced, how it felt to be running at the same time as I was there in my mind. My run was ten kilometres long and at the end of it I felt fantastic.

That day at work I made a conscious effort to remember as much of that meditation as I could. I used my mind power for good. When a stressful thing happened in my day I went back to watching those foxes play, using that memory to remember how good I felt. I try to remember that this is only work, and work is not my life. I let the stress just melt off me as I used my memories from my run and my meditation to relieve and free me.

The connection of mind and body is important and over time we forget that our bodies are nothing more than vessels that move us around. But in reality, our minds, bodies, and souls are all one in the same and learning to focus our mind power on other things then the past and the future or what we feel we have to do in life is an important skill to master. Building that connection between our minds and bodies is an enjoyable thing and being able to live in each moment when we want to is part of the whole experience.

Practicing meditation while we do physical things is part of building that connection between the three elements that make you, well, you. Below is a meditation called The Mountain Top. Enjoy this meditation for what it is and then try to use it the next time you are doing something physical; even better, burn the memory into your mind and use it throughout your day.

High on the Mountain Top

This morning while I was sitting in front of my pond with the waterfall gently calming me I thought about how life would be so much easier if I could cast away all of my worldly possessions, not have to work and just move to the top of a mountain. Just live a simple life. How good it would be to leave all the work stress and expectations behind. Let the outside world just melt away and just live a simple life where there are no deadlines, no ratios, no profit margins, no empty, meaningless things that we are told to place value on.

I thought about it and took a few deep breaths to clear my mind and started to think about what my cabin on the mountain top would look like.

(Before moving on, take the time to close your eyes and breath deep and slow, thinking about how nice it would be to have a cabin on the side of a mountain top and how it would feel to be completely free. Try to fully feel this, centre your mind and allow the emotions that you feel to fill you. Don't be afraid – just feel and recognize each emotion as you move forward in the meditation.)

Picture yourself waking up in a small wooded cabin on top of a mountain in the Canadian Rockies. Your first breath as you sit up in bed is filled with a mix of scents. The damp air mixed with the smell of hot coals still smoldering in the fire place from the night before, and the intoxicating smell of cedar fills the air. Your cabin is constructed of cedar and it is beautiful. You throw off your heavy handmade quilt and jump out of bed.

(Take the time to go there now, smell the cedar and the smoke. What does the blanket look like? Picture everything with great detail. The point of this meditation is to let the whole world disappear except for the cabin you are constructing with your mind.)

You walk over to the wooden counter and pick up your black cast iron kettle and then place it over the hot coals. You reach both of your hands overhead and stretch as far up as you can. *(Take your hands and stretch them above your head now, feel your back stretch out.)* Your back and sides thank you for this wake up call. You walk over to the front door and unlatch the rusty hinge. You swing the heavy wooden door open and walk outside. You turn to your left and see the morning sun rising.

(Picture the colours in your mind. Are there clouds? Is the sun big and orange? Is the sun mixing with the clouds to make a colourful backdrop? What can you smell? What do you hear?)

As you stand there you know that your neighbours are waking up also. The birds, foxes, bears, and all the other wildlife you are surrounded by are slowly getting up for the day. There is a morning mist floating on top of all the trees and sitting at the base of the mountain directly across from you, obscuring the view of the snowy top of this giant land mass you have the privilege of seeing every day.

(Picture the animals as they wake up. See this mountain in front of you. See the mist and watch it float by.)

You turn and walk over to your slate patio that you made by hand. You sit cross legged and just listen to what is going on around you.

(Breath deeply and imagine what you hear, is there pure silence? Or do you hear birds chirping, leaves rustling? Bring yourself there and experience it all.)

Out of your left ear you hear a chipmunk chatter. The neighbours are waking up! Then a "caw, caw!" sound off in the distance. The sun has risen and it is lighting up the forest and trees that appear to be about one kilometre away. They are glowing green. There are so many different shades of green visible in the light-drenched trees that you are in awe of this sight before you.

The patio is about three feet off the ground and sits perfectly on the edge of the cliff on the right hand side of the wooden cabin. There is a full 90-degree view of the valley below and the rushing river running through it. You have seen deer there drinking from the river and grazing on the lush green grass many times before. Bears fish in this river and you have seen them teaching their cubs how to catch fish. You have walked down there on numerous occasions to get water from the river and also to cool off with a swim on hot, summer days.

(What does this river look like? Picture the lush, green grass surrounding its bank. What does the shore line look like? Picture yourself down by the river. Imagine a mother bear frolicking with her cubs as they play and try to catch a fish.)

This morning the river is empty of wildlife, and you watch the mist slowly roll away exposing more of the river below and the white water rushing over a few large rocks. You look at the sky and it is deep blue, not a cloud to be seen. You uncross your legs and walk back into the cabin, pulling your kettle from the hot coal. You pour the scalding water into a coffee pot and go back out to the patio, sit down again and close your eyes. Take a few deep breaths in and out, just concentrating on your breathing. You are at peace and soon you smell that the coffee is ready. You walk back into the cabin and pour yourself a fresh cup. Taking your steaming mug with you, you return to your place on the patio, sitting with your legs folded under you. Enjoy the beauty that is all around you.

You now uncross your legs, reach forward and stretch to grab your toes. As you do this you relax your back and let it bend naturally.

(Do this move now and be careful not to strain yourself, but also allow yourself to fully commit to being in this moment as you stretch. Keep your eyes closed.)

After you finish this stretch, relax and sit comfortably. Have a sip of your coffee and look out into the wilderness. *(Truly see what you would like to see and the greater the detail the better.)*

The rest is up to you now. Feel free to discover and create your own story and ending. You can just sit and look around you and see the beauty, feel the emotions, the happiness of being so free in such a wonderful place. You can do more yoga poses, or perhaps even go for a walk down to the river. This is you cabin in the mountains and you can do what ever you'd like while you are staying there.

Once you are ready to leave the cabin I like to end the same way I started. Walk into the cabin and go to your bed, grab the heavy blanket and pull it over you. Then close your eyes and breath deep and slow taking your time to relax and enjoy the memories that are floating in your mind. When you are ready, open your eyes and you are back in reality.

I love this mountain top meditation because it is one of pure isolation and peace. So while I am at work and the day is getting stressful I think of that river, the mountains, maybe a deer grazing in the grass field leading down to the water. I see the whole scene and it brings a smile to my face. I will not let work control me or overwhelm me. I will smile and just go to my mountain top cabin and the world just fades away. Even if it is just for five minutes it is so nice to have this place to go to.

Bringing the physical movement into your meditations can heighten your experience in many ways. You can learn to meditate while you are on a walk by picturing yourself there and let the images resonate in your mind.

While you are working out, doing yoga, stretching, picture yourself on that patio doing your workout with those snowy topped mountains as your backdrop.

Whatever you prefer to do for exercise you can keep these images and memories alive and connect your mind and body in ways you never thought were possible.

I like keeping these images and feelings alive in my mind while I am running or doing yoga because it makes the time pass by quickly and keeps me looking forward to my next work out. While at work other people are running around and getting stressed about deadlines, problem customers, etc., I am using guided meditation to keep me calm and centered. It helps me to get my work done and stops any anxiety from coming to the surface. There are no ratios, percentages, or profit margins that have to be looked after. I will look after all that in due time but for now I am on the mountain and I will get to those things after, in a calm and controlled manner!

What a great place to go to! And what a great way to apply it to exercise and to work as well. Just because we have to be at work doesn't mean we can't have wonderful thoughts in our heads. How we use our mind power is up to us and no one can dictate what our thoughts are and how we use our minds.

Learn to combine your meditations with what you do physically throughout your day. Whether it is while you work out, walk, run, practice yoga, garden or even work, you will be giving yourself and your mind the love it deserves.

Next is another meditation in which I incorporate actual physical movement into the exercise. Don't worry if you cannot do what is written, just use your imagination and feel it in your mind instead. Remember to only do what is comfortable to you. If sitting somewhere comfortably is all you can manage then that is good enough. Read through what I have written and use your senses to bring yourself there. It is all about the detail and the mind power we all have, but learning to use body movement at the same time is the icing on the meditation cake.

Yoga on The Beach

A lot of times my meditations are memories I have from special times in my life. Times where I have ingrained the memory deep so I can never forget it, and I draw on it when I need to. Below is a memory I have from a run I completed while on vacation but I have changed it just a little bit and added myself driving up to the beach in a car. The rest of the images I have used are from the time I spent on the beach, taking in the sky, the sand, the waves, and all the details that I can remember from that experience.

Any time that you have a memory in your mind and you can picture yourself in that moment, that is an excellent way to build a meditation. If you really think about a memory you can actually get a pen and paper and make a list of what you see, what you smelled, how you felt, and capture all the emotions attached to that memory. Our minds are amazing and if you take the time to notice all these things you will realize just how powerful your mind is.

At the same time, however, nothing has to be real in a meditation. If you can imagine it – bringing yourself there using great detail – you are building a solid foundation. If you are lost in the moment, then you are accomplishing the goal.

For the next meditation, really try to concentrate on every detail and use your own memories of being on a beach. Use the images you have in your mind and insert them into the flow of what is happening. By doing this, you will bring this meditation to life.

If you took the time earlier to write down your experiences, see if you can add them into this meditation to make it truly unique to you.

(*Now take the time to fully relax, breathe slowly and focus your mind on your breathing. Let go of your thoughts and just pay attention to your chest moving up and then down with each breath you take. When you are completely relaxed, open your eyes and start to read below.*)

Imagine the most peaceful beach in the world. You drive up to it and park your car at the side of the road. You get out and look at the blue-green water.

(*What kind of car did you drive to the beach? And what does the sky look like, what can you smell?*)

The beach is calling you down to its white shore. You walk down a sand covered wooden boardwalk that stretches out to where the sand begins. You stop and remove your shoes and socks, looking to your left and then to your right. It is 7:00 a.m. and the beach is empty; it's all yours. Your heart leaps because you feel so good and happy, that this paradise is all yours to enjoy!

(*Breath in deep and picture this empty beach, feel your emotions as you are completely alone, you have this time to yourself.*)

The sun is at your back and you can feel its heat on you already, the day is young the sun is only beginning to rise. As you walk down to the shoreline your feet are getting a massage with every step you take.

The sand on top is warm from the sun shining on it, and as you push your weight down the sand gets cooler beneath your feet With every step you take you are treated to this new sensation as the sand feels different with every step.

(*Imagine what the sand feels like as you step into it. Feel the warmth of the top layer and then the cool of the sand below.*)

As you get closer to the water the sand gets harder and now you are standing on top of the sand, firm and wet and cool beneath your toes. (*Feel this sand on your feet, look out at the water and enjoy this moment for all it is worth.*)

You look to your left then your right and all you see is an empty beach. You place your right foot in the surf and wait for the water to gently roll up to meet it. The water rolls in and it is cool and refreshing so you take a full step forward and stand in the surf, letting the water calmly swoosh and surround your feet. You sink just a little bit into the sand. You close your eyes and let yourself feel the water around your feet as another burst of water comes and sinks you up to your ankles.

(*Allow yourself to feel this sensation as you sink into the sand. How does it feel? Try to let go, to be on the beach with your feet in the sand sinking slowly.*)

You extend both hands above your head and reach for the blue sky above you. You feel your back and shoulders stretch. Your upper back thanks you as you hold this stretch for 30 seconds. A calm, warm breeze comes in and brings a smile to your face.

(*Allow yourself to feel this sensation, even reach up above your head and make the mind and body connection.*)

You now step out of the water and turn walk toward the hard sand just outside of the water's reach. The sun warms the front of your body as you walk forward. You turn and face the water and breath deeply, taking in the fresh air.

(*Breathe deep now, feel each breath from the beginning inhale to the exhale. Feel the sun on your back, see the view in front of you, hear the water washing to the shore, smell the fresh air.*)

Looking out at the blue and green water in front of you, slowly sit cross legged in the sand.

(Just relax now and breathe as deep and long as you'd like, truly use your mind to picture this sight and spend as long as you'd like looking out at the water.

If you are not able to do these physical movements it is okay, just do the best you can. Building a connection with your mind and body is the goal here to truly getting lost in the moment.)

Now straighten both of your legs out in front of you, reach forward and grab your toes. Bend your lower back and stretch as far as you can, holding the position. As you do this look toward the water in front of you. Count to 30 inside your head and concentrate on your slow breathing at the same time, just looking out at the blue and green water in front of you.

When you reach 30 seconds and your breathing is deep and slow, release your pose and exhale for a full 10 seconds as you sit up.

The warmth of the sun is getting hotter on your back. You are calm and relaxed. Now take your right foot and place it on the inner thigh of your left leg. Again you reach both hands forward and grab your left foot, bending your back and stretching your side.

(Once again if you cannot do the movements that are described just do what you can or just picture yourself doing them.)

Count to 30 once again, breathing deeply, and look up at the wonderful sight above you. There are no clouds and the sky is a deep blue colour. Your breathing is deep and totally relaxed.

As you release the pose you exhale your full breath while you count to 10 in your head. Now you place you left foot on the inner thigh of you right leg and reach forward again, stretching your side as you bend your back and breath deeply. Watch the waves slowly roll on to the shore and hold for 30 seconds, breathing deeply and exhaling as you make the connection between mind and body. When you release this pose, you sit cross legged and look out at where the water meets the blue sky in front of you.

(As you look out at the image before you, take the time to experience each of the senses.)

The sun is now higher in the sky behind you, lighting up the water like never before. You now move to kneel in the sand and straighten your back, extending both hands to the sky and stretching as high as you can. Imagine you are trying to touch the blue sky above you, and hold this last pose for 30 seconds. Breathe deeper than you have ever breathed before, release the pose and go back to sitting cross legged in the damp sand.

(While you sit, just listen to all the different sounds around you. Take in all you can hear and feel, and recognize that this is true freedom.)

The sun is now hot and the breeze is picking up, the swooshing of the water slowly turning into small waves. The beach is now coming alive and soon people will be starting to show up. Families will be setting up their umbrellas and beach blankets, and soon children will be splashing in the waves and building sand castles.

(Imagine seeing the children playing, families setting up their gear along the beach. Imagine yourself there watching and maybe even playing in the sand, the joy and the happiness of being at the beach for the day!)

Now stand up and walk toward the water, or go for a run along the shoreline. While you are on your walk/run look at your surroundings and truly get lost in the moment.

(When you are finished, read below.)

Now that you are finished your walk or run and you are back where you started, you sit comfortably in the sand and cross your legs again. Breathe deeply and listen to the water, smell the wet sand and just enjoy the whole experience and what it has to offer you. Peace, calm, and happiness; you deserve all these feelings so take them in.

(Breathe deep, paying attention to your chest rising and falling.)

Stand up and take a good long look at the water and the sand, ingrain this scene into your mind so that you can go back to this place any time you would like. You now slowly walk back to your car. You walk up the wooden boardwalk, taking your time. This was your unique experience at the beach, so end it the way you want to.

(Give the end of this meditation all the time and feeling you can, do not feel rushed, feel comfortable and end when you'd like.)

The beach is a special place for me. I think of it as eye candy and ear candy; there are so many different ways you can draw on all of your senses with the sun, sand, water and the many sounds that you can hear. Taking the time to imagine this and make it the way you wish it to be is the most important part of this meditation. We all have different visions of what our perfect beach will look like, what the sand feels like under our feet. Enjoy the beach and transport yourself there in mind, body and soul. Let the world disappear and leave everything behind just for five or even fifteen minutes – you deserve it! We all do.

If you are able to do the three different yoga poses that I talked about in this meditation, then even better. To create a fully mind, body and soul experience is a great thing to accomplish. If you are not able to do the exercises then it doesn't matter just as long as you are able to bring yourself there in your mind. The next time you are out on a walk or run, breath deeply and bring yourself to that beach. Prepare yourself to be amazed at the power of your mind as you end up in two places at once: meditating on your peaceful beach, and walking or running here in this reality at the exact same time. This meditation will truly show you the power of your mind, body and soul.

Always remember that mistakes just don't exist when it comes to crafting your guided meditations because there is no wrong way to incorporate your own ideas. By making it your own using those personal experiences and expanding your mind, you are freeing your soul.

Turning Vacation Into a State of Mind

People love to get away on vacation, and I don't think there are any exceptions to this. I don't really know of anyone who doesn't love a good vacation. The feeling of taking time to care for yourself, getting away and leaving behind work responsibilities and all your troubles is almost necessary for a person's well-being. Just actually being free to be yourself and do things you love is such a wonderful feeling and we all need to do it.

I had always struggled with leaving work thoughts behind when I went away on vacation. I always had something on my mind, and it was always there just in the background. Even when I was in the middle of playing with my son I could never quite just let go of my normal everyday life. I found eventually that over time while I was on vacation those thoughts would slowly fade away and I was able to fully enjoy my vacation time, leave work and the world behind. I found the experience of being on vacation to be one of the greatest feelings, because you take the time to treat yourself to good and enjoyable things, you relax and you truly love your experience and in doing so love yourself and treat yourself properly.

I decided to take all these good feelings and turn it into a meditation! This way, I could relive all the good things that I had experienced while I was on vacation. Vacation doesn't have to be a place you go to, but it can be a state of mind! For this meditation I chose to go up north to a cottage in the woods.

I am not sure what it is about going up north into the forest but some of my most memorable vacations were spent in wooded cabins on lakes or rivers. Spending time with my family or friends and making time for myself in the mornings to do things I love brings a smile to my face. Sitting together as a group, playing games, swimming, going on boat rides, fishing – whatever it is you truly enjoy doing, you can take those feeling with you and you can make them real in a meditation.

The next meditation we are going to do is called Down on the Dock. It is very peaceful and very self-indulgent. You will have to really draw on all five of your senses and the more detail you can use the greater the experience will be. Turn your mind up to 11 and bring yourself fully and completely down to the dock with me!

Down on the Dock

Every year I go to a cottage in the woods with my family, and it's about a 6 hour drive away from where I live. It is a peaceful drive on a two lane highway, kind of like a country road. It's not a three or four lane super highway with speeding cars, the honking of horns, and people following too close. This highway goes through small towns and is a winding road, which has many hills and valleys with creeks and green, grassy fields. There are farms along the way as well with horses and cows grazing in lush old pastures. To say the drive there is an enjoyable experience is the absolute truth, a laid back drive that is beautiful and just as relaxing as being at the cottage.

(*Breathe deeply now, make sure that you are comfortable and relax yourself fully. Picture yourself now in your car driving on this highway, you're not in a hurry and the windows are down, the sun is shining. Who is with you? What music do you have playing on the radio? Bring yourself there now. Take your time as you are on vacation and there is no hurry for you to get to your destination – in fact, the drive is part of the vacation itself*)

The cottage is in the middle of a dense forest, the road to the cottage about two kilometres off the highway. The road is gravel and windy and you have to drive slowly to navigate the rocky turns and mossy slick shoulders. There is a sign at the entrance to this road that lists your last name and cottage way.

(Picture yourself now turning off the main country highway and driving on this road. Imagine everything: the sun shinning through the trees, the sound of your car tires slowly going over the gravel, etc.)

There's one last steep hill right at the end of the road that leads to the cottage, and you have to give the car all the gas you've got to make it up. The tires spin and the gravel flies, hitting the underside of the car as you rocket up the last hill and once you are at the top, the cottage is just a sharp turn to your left and you are there.

(Feel the excitement of reaching your final destination, the exaltation of making it up the hill and now knowing that you are just seconds from parking the car at the cottage.)

As you make the turn into the driveway you see the red log cottage and you smile. The cottage has two bedrooms with a breathtaking view of the lake. It is a bungalow, nothing fancy, and nestled away in the woods it is nice and comfortable just for you.

(What does the cottage look like? Picture it as you drive up. What do the trees look like? What does the driveway look like? Picture everything as you drive up to your cottage.)

Once you pull up, you get out of your car and take a deep breath, filling your lungs with the fresh air, so crisp and clean compared to the city air. You close your car door and follow the path around back of the cottage: there will be time to unpack later. Right now you want to see the lake! As you reach the back of the cottage you make a left hand turn, and stop to look out at this beautiful sight.

(Now use all five of your senses and bring yourself right to this moment, breathe deeply and just enjoy this sight for what it is.)

There is a large deck on the back of the cottage with comfortable chairs and a large table in the centre for you to put a drink on or play cards, or even light candles for a stargazing night. This back porch is entertainment central at the cottage. The table is made out of a large tree cut in half and sanded and finished perfectly.

(*Picture this table and the back porch as you would like to, use as much detail as you can and make it a real place.*)

As you sit on the deck you look out on the lake through the trimmed pine trees. The sight lines are perfect and you can see the entire lake. (*What do you see and hear as you look out at the lake?*)

Leading off the deck is a well-worn trail in the sandy ground, and it is framed by rocks on either side of the trail. This trail leads down to the dock at the lake's shoreline. (*Walk down to the trail now and go to the dock.*)

The dock is big – fifty feet wide by fifty feet deep and is made out of cedar (which smells intoxicating in the early morning when there is a fresh coat of dew intensifying the scent.)

(*Picture this dock now and see yourself stepping onto it and looking around at the wonderful view. It is breathtaking.*)

You turn and walk back up to the car to unpack and settle in for a good night's sleep. It has been a long but enjoyable ride.

(*Now you are free to picture the cottage on the inside as best as you can, make it look, smell, and feel the way you want it to. Feel you are now there completely and the only thoughts you have are about this cottage, this wonderful place you have created.*)

The next morning you wake up early, turn the coffee maker on and make your way down to the dock. This is the best part of your day, and how you like to start every day when you are up at the cottage.

You love going down to the dock in the early mornings just before the sun rises. The silence is pure and absolute, not a sound other than the water swishing up on the rocky shore, not an aggressive swoosh but a calm one that happens every two or three seconds. It is dark but not night time dark, just enough light to feel comfortable. You sit right at the end of the dock and watch the mist slowly roll by about a foot off the lake's edge and three feet above the water. It moves slowly, creating ghostly shapes before your eyes. The sun rises and begins to light up the whole scene; the lake is about to come to life.

(Take the time now to see this mist roll by, hear the water swooshing up against the rocky shoreline.)

The lake is about five kilometres wide and there are pine trees lining the shoreline. The sunrise is slowly lighting up the sky, and your eyes are being treated to a multicoloured landscape of greens and yellows and browns. *(See the sun rising slowly, peeking over the treetops and bringing the landscape to life.)*

There are cottages that dot the shoreline, some are even hidden in the green hills. As it gets brighter and brighter around you, the mist slowly dissipates and you hear a loon call from off in the distance. Life is beginning to wake up in front of your waiting eyes and ears.

Take a deep breath and let nature slowly come to life, take in everything as if you are seeing it for the first time.)

You hear a fish jump out of the water. You look over to your right and watch the ripples in the water expand and slowly disappear before your eyes. You look over to your left and see the loon you heard calling just moments before dive down into the depths of the lake, perhaps going after the fish that just jumped. After about twenty seconds the loon emerges from the water not far in front of you with a large splash. It caught a fish. The fish is flopping around in its tightly closed bill. The loon flaps its wings and is airborne with its morning catch, maybe flying off to feed awaiting babies or just landing somewhere to enjoy the catch alone.

You look into the clear, tea coloured lake right in front of the dock and you can see to the bottom.

(*What do you see as you look into the clear water; are there fish swimming? A turtle passing by on its morning swim? Create any images you may want to see.*)

The lake is coming alive as the sun rises. Birds start chirping, and the water is now swooshing up on the rocks, getting louder and faster as there is now a calm breeze. You take a deep breath and you smell freshly brewed coffee coming from the cottage. You stand up take a good look at the view before you. Now you make your way up the sandy path to the cottage. You go inside and pour yourself a steaming mug of coffee. You then go back outside and sit facing the breathtaking view in front of you.

(*Take the time now to relax, breathe deeply and truly embrace this feeling and the freedom you have in this moment.*)

The rest of this meditation is up to you, take the time now to make the ending your own and realize that there will be many more trips to this cottage, down to the dock, and that each trip can be different.

This meditation is one I enjoy very much. I can create so many different experiences down on the dock. Children diving into the water and playing while I sit with my wife and friends enjoying their company... candlelit dinners on the back deck, star watching on the dock late at night. If you can think of it, you can transport yourself there. The opportunity to bring in all the senses to this experience is never ending. You can draw on sight, sound and smell so very easily because being up north is such a wild and untamed place, the sky is the limit with this meditation.

After this meditation I am always refreshed and relaxed; work is gone and the rest of my day is filled with memories of being down on the dock. The most important thing is my state of mind after this meditation – I am in such a state of relaxation that it is only matched by actual being there physically. The power of meditation is so incredible, I can carry my memories throughout an entire day and the hours pass by faster because I am happy and still at the cottage in my mind.

It can become a little secret that you keep to yourself, you can have a little smirk on your face all day because while the world is spinning in its usual way because you have these memories still fresh in your mind. You do your work and all along you're really sitting on that dock doing whatever you want to be doing and you're the only one who knows it! That is what life is about, and happiness and meditation is a doorway to that feeling!

Remembering that the feelings you have when on vacation are created by you, you are also able to feel that way in any moment in your life. It is so very important to realize vacation can be a state of mind. I encourage you to practice this meditation as much as you can until it feels natural and you make every image yours and yours alone. Having a vacation state of mind will help you enjoy your day and keep you grounded even when you think it may be impossible. Meditation is something that you carry with you throughout the day and doesn't end when the meditation ends.

Creating A Safe Place

(Taken from Creative Writing for the Mind,
Body & Soul and Why I Run)

A safe place is somewhere you can go to in your mind to escape the outside world, calm yourself and help stop you from being triggered into a downward spiral. This is different from guided meditation which we have been practicing and enjoying in this book. It is different because this will be a place which will always be the same every time. You will learn to bring yourself there whenever you'd like to. The idea behind it is that you will ingrain the details in your mind in such a way that you will make it a completely personal experience. You will be able to bring yourself there quickly and with very little effort.

You will use all the tools which you put into practice when writing your own guided meditations and also practicing the ones in this book as well. You will create a safe place just for you. Before we get started, I would like to share how I found my safe place, and then we will learn to create your own safe place. A place to have and love and go to when you feel the need to. But even better than that, a place where you can go and feel good about yourself and your accomplishments, because having a special place that is unique and just for you is a great accomplishment unto itself.

The following is an excerpt from Why I Run, detailing how I found my own safe place.

Journal entry:

I need to talk to my therapist about why I can't let go of my emotions, why I just can't be free from my thoughts. How there are always things on my mind. I never truly relax and just let go.

I am afraid when I do I'll just cry and cry and cry, and just explode with emotion. I have already done that when I wasn't even close to being completely relaxed. What's going to happen to me when I truly let go and let my emotions free after all these years? I am scared and terrified of that moment. I need to feel. I need to be free. I need to let go. I need to be me!! I need to go to this safe place and just let whatever happens happen.

What will happen? I am scared.

I was still spiraling and my therapist wanted to install a safe place that I could go to in my head, like a kind of meditation, to calm me down and make me stable again. Somewhere I could just be at peace.

Now the struggle started. I was so nervous about it I could not relax at all. I was convinced that it was just not going to happen. I could never create a safe place.

It was up to me to find my safe place, so I started.

Attempt #1

I pictured myself walking Moe, my dog who I have recently put sleep, to the park, us playing Frisbee. The sun was shining and there were pine trees lining the right side of the park and I could smell the morning dew and Moe was running and catching the Frisbee. I could feel the grimy dog saliva on my hand from throwing the Frisbee. I could hear Moe's teeth bite down and catch it as I threw it.

But picturing that didn't work. I could not go there. I could not relax and really I wasn't over Moe at all. The experience was a total disaster. I just broke down and was a mess. I was failing at another thing in life: I was not able to install a safe place and I had never come to grips with putting my dog to sleep...

So it was back to the drawing board for round two at the safe place...

Attempt #2

This time I was at the beach sitting on a beach chair and the sun was shining. It was hot. I was having a beer and the water was just washing up on the shore, nice and calm. My son Dylan was swimming and my wife Sherri was beside me. It was great that my therapist was able to bring me there without a problem at all. But the last time I was at the beach was when I had just started therapy and I had a major break down and I ended up just thinking about that day and again I broke down and was a mess once again. I was a failure all over again.

Here is the Journal entry from that time at the beach when I actually broke down.

Journal entry:

At the beach

I hate my life. I'm trying to get better but wife Sherri is so angry and hates me for what I'm going through. What's the use anyway? I'm just going to keep living the way I'm living, unhappy and acting the whole time. So I don't hurt her and Dylan.

That day at the beach I fell apart in front of Sherri, tears and everything. She saw me at the worst.

I was going to break for real. I told her that sometimes I wish I was gone. I wish I would disappear. I told her that I'm not happy, that I have been acting for years and that I'm going crazy. I just fell apart. I was crying and shaking and I just spiraled down. What a way to spend our last days of vacation.

Attempt #3

So now it was time again to try something new. But my therapist just wanted to work on relaxation in general and so she introduced me to the tree meditation, which is now one of my favourite things to do. I sit and breathe deep and just feel how my body is sitting and just notice everything that is around me. I close my eyes and just breathe deeply. She asks me what kind of tree I see before me. I tell her I see a large brown maple tree. I walk toward this tree and I magically just step into it and just breathe, breathe deeply. I slowly bring the air in through the leaves and push it down through my trunk and out into the ground through my roots and then in through my roots and out through my leaves. I just imagine I can feel the wind blowing me from side to side and I let my body move freely as this tree, just feeling relaxed and peaceful. She asks me what I am feeling, what emotions are flowing through me and I tell her and she just says go with that feeling and enjoy it for as long as you like. Then when you are feeling just right take a deep breath and step out of the tree and open your eyes slowly and stay in that emotion you were feeling. I open my eyes and step out and I am relaxed and at peace and holy smokes I feel so good.

Guess what? I found my safe place and it was fantastic!

I have grown the tree meditation into a beautiful, safe place. I go there all the time. It is so peaceful and I don't cry. I feel free and I can do whatever I like and I just step into the tree.

The tree is a perfectly safe place. When I need to go there, I walk around the tree and run my hand over its bark, feeling its roughness and its nooks and crannies, and kind of say "Hi" to this tree. I imagine that I have this gift and I just slowly walk into this tree and I feel its whole circulatory system and as I breathe, I take the air in through the leaves and out through the roots. I feel the sap coursing through my limbs and I imagine the wind blowing my leaves around. I just feel everything the tree feels, like birds landing on me and even building nests and having baby birds living on me. I stay in the tree until I feel I have stayed long enough and whatever caused me to be stressed out has left my mind. The outside world can't touch me here. I am free from everything in the tree and that is so, so special.

When I walk out, I thank the tree and I give it a nice pat and once again rub my hand along its trunk to feel its bark and roughness. I walk away relaxed and complete and I take the tree's strength with me as I leave my special safe place.

I had over analyzed the safe place until I was terrified of it and I had all these expectations and worries about what a safe place was. A safe place is just that, a safe place, end of story. No over thinking and I can cry, I can feel whatever I want to because it's my safe place!

Thank you, Mastora, for my safe place.

We will learn to create our own safe place. We will move slowly through each step, we will write out each step in a journal and slowly build our own safe place. If you don't have a journal go out and get one. You may also use a tablet, a phone, a laptop, or computer. Whichever platform you choose you must feel comfortable and free to express yourself.

Creating Your Own Safe Place

Step 1: The Name

A safe place cannot be given to someone. I cannot create one for you, you have to make it yourself. But what I can do is give you the tools to build your own. We are going to go through the steps one at a time and you will learn to create your own safe place. It is going to be fun and all you will need is a book to write in. Let's get started.

The first thing you need to do to create this safe place is to write down some places you might have in mind. Take your time and write freely. You can choose many things, for example: a place in time that you felt good in, an activity that you enjoy doing, a good memory you may have from the past, or time spent with a friend.

Here are some additional examples:

- Sitting on the beach

- Ice skating
- Swimming in a lake or pool
- Flying like a bird
- A bike ride with a friend or by yourself
- Exercising, running, walking, playing a sport, etc.

Once you have picked from your list, name it! Make it yours and yours alone. By naming it you enforce the memory of going there. Just saying the name will remind you of the place and the feelings you have when you are there. Whenever I say my tree I have a mental image and I automatically breathe deeper and feel myself relax. That is how powerful your safe place can be.

Step 2: Use Your Senses

Bringing in the senses just like we did when writing out a guided meditation, think about the main things you want to draw on from this place.

Example:
Riding my bike.

Sight

- What does the bike look like? Is it old or new?
- What colour is it? (Don't be afraid to make it any colour you would like)
- What do you see while you are riding?
- Where are you riding to? Write about it.

Describe everything you see in great detail.

Sound
What do you hear?
- Is the bike noise?
- Birds chirping

Feel
- Can you feel the wind as you ride?

- Is the road bumpy?
- What do the handle grips feel like?
- Is it hard or easy to pedal
- Does it steer easily?

Smell

- Describe any scent in the air
- Is someone barbecuing?
- The smells after a fresh rain

Taste

- Do you have a drink holder? What type of drink do you have on your bike?
- Is your mouth dry from the wind as you ride?

Using your five senses, you can bring your safe place alive. The more detail, the better, and it will be easier for you to reach this safe place.

Step 3: Making It Real

Write your safe place out and as you write it down, take the time to completely go there. Start with relaxing and breathing deeply like when we are doing a guided meditation. When you are relaxed, write out your title and just think about it for a while. Put yourself there mentally and picture it as if it were a real place.

When you have this picture in your mind, write out how you would like it to start. When you are finished writing, stop and go over what you wrote three times and then close your eyes. Picture yourself going there.

Once you are there, write the body of your safe place using the details you wrote out in step two as much as you can. Pay attention to how you are feeling emotionally as you do this and notice how your body is relaxed and free of stress. As you write, concentrate on the good, happy feelings you are having as you create this safe place. Don't rush through this stage of writing and take as many breaks as you'd like.

Once you have the body written, start reading from the top of the page and make sure that as you read you are going there and seeing and feeling everything you have written. Once you have done this, write out how you would like it to end. As you write this out, again, pay attention to your emotions and notice how free and happy you are as you write your ending.

Once you are finished this exercise read it over again and make sure that this is your safe place and you are comfortable in it. Love your safe place and think about it as you finish up reading.

Step 4: Putting It Into Practice

Now that you have your safe place written out and you have read it over and over again, you will now put it into practice. Each morning when you wake up, you will go somewhere quiet and open you journal. Breathe deeply and relax yourself, then you will read through your safe place from beginning to end, taking your time to really go there in mind and body. Once you are done you will close the book and again go there in mind and body, this time noticing all your emotions and how your body feels while there. Once you are finished, go about your day as you normally would, but keep your safe place on your mind; even just saying the title every once in a while will help to keep you calm and centred.

At lunch time you will start your lunch by closing your eyes and going to your safe place, this will only take you maybe 2 or 3 minutes to do, then eat your lunch and enjoy it. Once you are finished eating, go to your safe place again.

Have you ever heard the saying "whistle while you work?" For the after-noon while you work, just in the back of your mind, think about your safe place as you go about your day. Notice how you can carry the good emotions with you that accompany your safe place and notice how you can be completely relaxed as you go through your second half of the day. Realize just how wonderful having a safe place can be.

At the end of your day, before you go to bed, reread your journal entry and allow your mind to travel to that safe space again. Make sure that you are allowing yourself to commit to this exercise one hundred percent, and when you are done you can put the book down and end your night.

You are to do this exercise every day for a week and enjoy the time you spend doing it. Sooner or later this safe place will become second nature to you, and will be an automatic and natural response to stress.

Step 5: Using Your Safe Place

Now that you have your safe place and you are able to go to it with ease and without struggling, you can start applying it!

I use my safe place when I feel I am getting overwhelmed, like I really can't control my emotions. When I am at work and the job I am doing just seems like a task I will never finish, or when it is late at night and I just can't sleep and my mind is cycling over and over, my safe place calms me every time.

Your safe place is yours alone and it is meant to relax you when you feel that you need to take yourself out of a bad situation. Your safe place is there for you always and it is up to you to determine when and how you use it.

Here is an example of how I used my safe place on a run, taken from my novel Why I Run.

Thought record:
On my run this morning.
I am so proud of myself today and I am not afraid to show it. I am happy and proud. This morning on my run I spent my time in my safe place.
Moods:
Relaxed 100%, happy 100%
Sit:
I went to my safe place. My safe place is a tree. I imagined that I was a tall tree planted in my parents' back yard. My father's ginkgo tree he planted when I was just six years old. I breathed deeply, inhaling through my leaves and exhaling through my roots. I just relaxed and did this for quite a while. Just thinking about what it must be like to be a tree. Not to have any expectations

or worries, to have nothing to do but grow and grow, because I am a tree and that's what trees do.

I picture my father as a strong, young man planting me with his strong and caring, gentle hands. They are the same strong hands that held me as a baby and rocked me to sleep. They rocked my six older brothers as well. I think about how my father would water me after work and just stand there watching everyday as I grew.

As this tree I also watch a family grow around me never wanting to interfere or pass judgment or criticize, wanting only to breathe deeply and grow nice and slow, and watch this family grow as well. I watch soccer games. I watch this strong man build tree houses for his sons. I watch him play baseball with them and even build a pool and ice rinks for hockey games.

All along, my branches just grew and grew. I got taller and taller, children turned to teens and teens turned to men. The man who was once so strong also got older and older, and became a grandfather.

As a tree, time must be a very peaceful thing. As a tree, I just watch life flow by, with no obligations and no commitments. I just grow and learn just like I am doing in real life, growing and learning how to be myself. I love my safe place and I love who I am.

This was a goal I had made ever since I started therapy and found my safe place, which was not an easy task at the time. Now I am proud of myself, which is something I really haven't been able to say ever. I am proud because I did this. I reached a meditative state went to my safe place. ran 8km in my safe place, my tree. I am proud of myself because I have this safe place I can go to. I am worth changing and I am not afraid to be myself.

Enjoy your safe place.

Now I will share my safe place with you. This is one of my many journeys to my tree. Read through it and enjoy as I share my most intimate and cherished place.

The Tree (My safe place)

My tree meditation is my safe place and it is the most peaceful place in my world. I go there all the time when I get stressed out, when I feel overwhelmed, and when I need to just get away from the outside world. I use my safe place at night when my mind is racing all over the place and I can not sleep. Going to my tree focuses my thoughts and afterwards I will drift off to sleep.

I even use it when I just feel like being happy and treating myself to quiet and familiar place. Meditation isn't always about escaping, it is about self care and love. It is about taking care of yourself and enjoying the power of your mind. We spend so much energy worrying, over thinking and just wasting our mind power. Doing all these meditations and learning how to use our minds for our own enjoyment is such a wonderful thing. After all, we are not here just to be stressed out people. We are here to enjoy life.

I will now share my tree meditation with you! Start with going somewhere that you are comfortable and relaxed. Start to breathe deeply and when you are ready, read below and slowly take yourself into the tree meditation.

The Tree

Find a place that is truly peaceful and sit down. Make sure that you are one hundred percent comfortable and breathe deeply. As you do this, take the time to feel your breath flowing through you. From the moment it enters your body, until it travels down into your lungs, feel the end of the breath as you are now filled with air. Release your breath and feel it as it leaves your body. Repeat this breathing until you are fully relaxed. Once you are, read below.

Picture yourself walking on a path through a forest, the path covered with cedar chips and winding straight through the heart of the forest. As you walk down the path you can see far off in the distance that there is a clearing at the end and then nothing but green grass.

(Picture what this path looks like, smell the cedar as you walk, each step you take releasing the intoxicating smell. Try to envision how dense the forest is as you walk- what do you hear? Are there birds chirping? Squirrels running about? What wild life do you see and hear? Is the sun shining through the forest, is it warm or hot? Now is the time to bring this meditation to life.)

As you get close to the end of the path you see a wide open field that is encircled by more forest. it is like someone cut a three kilometre long oval out of the forest and planted the most deeply coloured green grass in the middle. You look to your left and to your right and there is nothing but tall trees around you, almost like a wall, protecting the green grass.

(As you look to your right and left picture what this place looks like, try to feel the solitude and the peaceful feeling that is created by this open space.)

You now turn to your right and walk along the tree line that is so well groomed it is like a gardener has been looking after the entire green space. Up ahead you see your tree, and it is tall and mighty.

(Picture what this tree might look like from a distance as you walk up to it. What colour is it? What do its leaves look like? Try to see it standing before you.)

As you get closer you now see the true size of the tree: its trunk is 6 feet around and its roots are massive as they sprawl out in all directions. The trunk is tall and the bottom branches are 6 feet off the ground. You walk up to your old friend and walk around its wondrous mass. You run your hand over its granny bark, you feel the differenttextures; you are saying hi to the tree and it is welcoming you.

(Now take the time to say hi to the tree, run your hand along its bark, feel it and experience it. Feel the tree's strength and take the time to notice it's energy as you run your hand along its sides.)

Now that you have said hi to the tree, you take a deep breath and let it out. You take another deep breath and let it out again. You reach forward with both your hands now and with yet another deep breath your hands magically disappear into the tree. You continue to walk forward and pass directly into the tree.

(Take the time now to do this walk into the tree. What does it feel like to pass into this tree, how does it feel to be in the centre of this huge tree? What emotions are you feeling? What do you see as you adjust to being in the tree?)

You now take a deep breath and as you let it out, you can feel the trees life and energy. You slow your breath to match the tree's movement of oxygen. You now sit down and cross your legs as you continue to match the tree's breathing and how its circulatory system is working. You are drawing oxygen in through the leaves and down into the trunk and into the roots. You feel everything as you breathe, and you become one with the tree.

(Breathe now, in through your leaves, feel the movement from the top to the bottom. Feel oxygen passing down and into the ground and back again. Do not rush this, allow yourself to become one with the tree, you are creating a bond of friendship and trust with this tree. Nothing can harm you when you are here. The tree always welcomes you to become one with it.)

As you breathe with the tree you are now one with it, you are now feeling everything the tree feels. If it is raining you feel the rain, you feel it cool your leaves on a hot day. If it is hot you feel the sun hitting your leaves and warming you. If a bird lands on you, you feel at as well. Even birds building nests and having families, you feel it all and you enjoy it.

(*Imagine what all those sensations would feel like and picture the birds in their nest, feel the heat from the sun and enjoy the cooling effect of the rain hitting your leaves. Become this tree and experience it all. Take some time now and let your mind wander, see the world as the tree.*)

When you are in the tree you are able to see all around you – a full 365 degree view – and the sights you have seen are so memorable. You can watched deer grazing on the wonderful green grass. You have watched rabbits pop up from their holes and sneak out to eat the foliage along the forest edge. Baby foxes playing under the shade of your branches- you see it all. As a tree you are always present and see so much and grow everyday both in mind and body.

(*Take the time to now experience any and all of these wonderful things, watch the deer grazing and bring in as much detail as you can to make it feel real. Watch the foxes and feel the freedom they have, as they truly have not a care in the world while they play. This is your tree time and you can see it all, feel it all and love it all. Nothing is out of the question when you create your own experiences!*)

As you fully explore the tree meditation, also think about what a tree might feel as it grows everyday, stronger and stronger. A tree does not question what is happening to it but it embraces it, it welcomes everything that happens to it and around it. It trusts that everything in its life will just flow, it doesn't want to control anything but just enjoy what it experiences without question.

(*Take the time now to breathe with the tree, in through its leaves and out through the trunk, in through the trunk and out through the leaves. Truly get lost in this moment of being free and as strong as the tree*).

You have enjoyed your time inside the tree and now you will try to take one strong memory from this experience with you as you stand up and take a step forward out of the tree. Once you are out, turn around and say goodbye to the tree. Walk around it again and run your hand over its bark and give it a nice pat.

(Say goodbye now in your own way; the tree will always be there for you anytime you need it!)

As you walk away from the tree, take a good look around you and remember all you can. You walk up the path through the woods and you take a deep breath as you walk along the peaceful trail leading back to your car.

(Try now to imagine this with as much detail as you can. Each piece of this safe place meditation can be carried with you throughout your day.)

You reach the end of the trail and see your car waiting to take you away. Think about my safe place and what you would like to carry with you from it. I hope you have enjoyed my tree, my safe place. I hope you were able to use all your senses and in doing so made some memories of your own.

Using your mind and the power you have to bring all the senses into a meditation is the key to truly unlock your mind's power. The greater the detail, the fuller the experience will be.

Using Great Detail

Using great detail enhances our meditations and also lets us create great memories to carry on throughout our days. Learning to focus that over-active mind and using the power to bring each detail to life is the goal. I have said it before in this book and I will say it again, I believe that most people who struggle with depression and anxiety are some of the most brilliant and smart people in the world, they just were never taught to use their minds for something good. But instead they used overthinking to hinder their lives. We lose sleep and our minds actually work against us.

The next meditation is a perfect example of when I just couldn't shut down. I was overthinking everything that was happening in my life, so I decided to take this energy and focus it on something else altogether. I thought to myself, where did my tree come from? How did it grow? As my thoughts raced, I decided to come up with a meditation called "the seed." Everything has a starting point, so why not make up a beginning for my tree? A history, if you will, a background to how it came to be.

So I created the seed meditation which puts into practice the use of great detail to deepen the meditative state and truly show just how powerful are minds can be.

Humans by nature are very curious creatures and want to know where things come from and how things begin. This meditation I call "The Seed" came about because I was curious about my tree, my safe place. I wanted to create a backstory to my tree and experience what it was like for my tree

78

to grow from a seed. This really expanded my mind and got me to use even more detail, helping focus my mind like never before.

We can learn so much from a simple thing that just grows and grows, sometimes for hundreds of years. The nature of a tree is to just grow and not to question, not to judge but to trust that everything will be okay. This meditation taught me to trust, to let go of control, and to realize that my place in the world is right where I am at that given moment and happiness is in my possession. I make it myself and I can find ways of being happy even when I don't have control. Realizing I don't need to be in control actually put me in complete control of my life, ironically.

Enjoy this meditation, put yourself in each moment, and instead of thinking of the past or future just live in the now. Grow with the seed into your own tree.

- Be patient and go slow, read and then close your eyes and put yourself there. Use all your senses

- Never feel rushed but do the opposite – when you feel anxious, pull back and just notice that feeling and let it pass

- Enjoy this time and be creative

Below is the seed meditation I built. Read it through and follow the instructions as always, then make it your own.

The Seed

This morning on my run I thought to myself, where did my tree come from? How did it grow into such a large and stable place? I started to picture just how this tree I go to all the time started its life.

A seed is a fragile thing, so special and delicate. It is energy just waiting for the right conditions to happen to bring it to life. How a seed gets planted can happen in many ways: a person can dig a hole and gently place it in the ground and carefully cover it with dirt, then nurture it until it sprouts and grows. Taking care to water it daily and watch over it will cause the seed to grow and grow.

It can also be blown by the wind, dropped by an animal, or fall from a tree and make its way into the ground. There it gets nurtured by nature itself, watered and taken care of in a natural way. Either way the seed needs to be put into the earth and once there the magic happens.

(How was your seed planted? Close your eyes and picture how you would like your seed to grow. Where is your seed planted? In forest? In a field where it will grow and become a symbol of strength standing alone by itself? Or maybe in your backyard where you water it and take care of it, protect it and love it.)

Once in the earth, the seed starts to feel comfortable and it sends out a tiny root. It doesn't question why, it just trusts that it is the right thing to do.

(What does your root look like? Imagine the feeling of the root pushing out and finding its way into the earth.)

Shortly after its root hits the earth, a tiny, fragile sprout makes its way out from the seed.

(What does your sprout look like? Picture it and notice everything about it. How does it feel to be this sprout pushing itself out of the seed and then through the earth? Be this sprout and feel what it is like to start life.)

This sprout is tiny and could be broken very easily but it has no fear, it only knows one thing, that its job is to grow and it does it without thinking or second guessing.

The sprout feels the warmth of the sun and it enjoys the feeling of being warmed by its rays, never questioning where the sunlight came from or why it is there, only that it feels good to have warmth.

(Breathe deeply now and feel the sunlight warming you, it is like a warm blanket and it comforts you.)

The sunlight sparks the sprout into sending out a tiny limb and this limb grows a tiny leaf. Again, the sprout doesn't question its growth it just grows, and nothing will stop the sprout from growing. Sometimes the sun doesn't shine and it rains but the sprout doesn't fear that the sun will not return, it just enjoys the rain and the break from the sun.

(Feel the rain washing over you, feel the water soaking into the ground and reaching your root, enjoy the feeling of taking this water in through your root- it feels natural and you enjoy it.)

When it rains the sprout stretches to meet the raindrops. It enjoys the feel of the water running over its leaf and down its fragile sprout body, into the ground. After a while the sprout sends out another tiny limb and a grows another leaf.

(Feel what it must be like to grow this new limb, imagine the feeling of pushing the limb out and the making a wonderful green leaf. What does the leaf look like? Picture the leaf in great detail.)

Over time, the once-tender skin of the sprout turns into a hard brown skin. The sprout grows taller. This sprout is now a sapling and knows its job is to grow and grow. The sapling trusts that it is doing the right thing, in fact it knows it is doing the right thing and is confident and shows it by growing straight up into the sky.

(Feel the confidence of the sapling, feel the emotions of knowing who you are and that nothing is going to stop you now from growing.)

The sapling's leaves drink in the sunlight and a sense of strength is there like never before.
(Imagine how it must feel to have the sun warming your leaves. What are the sensations you experience?)

The sapling starts to feel its circulatory system and knows that it is doing the right thing by embracing its new growth and new feelings of being part of nature. It now sends out many roots that drink up the rain water and the moisture deep in the ground. This sapling is embracing its strength and growing and causing change within itself.

(Take the time now to picture this sapling and the feelings it must have as it starts to feel its circulatory system, taking air in through the leaves and down through its trunk, into the roots and back again. Feel the strength you have as you are growing bigger and experiencing new things everyday.)

The sapling is now two feet tall and is growing faster and faster, sending out more limbs and growing more leaves. The sapling's once tiny, twiggy trunk is now getting thick and brown. Its skin is now turning into hard bark. This sapling is thriving and becoming a small tree, standing straight and confident, beaming with life. The colour of its leaves are bright green and this tree is truly happy in its home, deeply rooted and enjoying life.

One day it notices that the sun is not as hot as it once was, now the nights are cold and the wind is not as warm as it once was.

(Feel how this small tree is experiencing its new environment, how strong and trusting it is. Feel the difference in the shifting of the seasons and how the tree doesn't fight it but is a part of it instead.)

The tree starts to notice that its once green leaves are turning different colours and they no longer feel the sun like they once did. The tree doesn't panic, it just trusts that what is happening is right and that whatever happens, everything will be okay.

Why wouldn't nature look after it? Everything that has happened so far in the tree's life has felt good, even though at times it felt uncomfortable and foreign the tree always expected that everything was going to be okay in the end. The tree just lets time pass and trusts that what is happening is right. Soon all the leaves have turned brown, red and yellow, and the wind blows them off its now strong limbs. This now medium sized tree is experiencing a new season: fall.

(Put yourself there and imagine it fully and completely, feel what it must feel like to completely trust that what is happening is right. Also feel the leaves gently fall off your limbs, picture them slowly falling and hitting the ground.)

The tree is now feeling like it must sleep. The sun is no longer warm and the tree goes dormant. The tree knows it is alright to do so. It doesn't question how or why, it just knows that it is the right thing to do, so the tree goes to sleep.

The winter is long and cold but one day the tree slowly wakes up and soon it feels the sun again, like meeting an old friend. The tree welcomes its warmth and remembers how it felt and how it nurtured the tree.

(Imagine how it must feel to wake up from a long sleep and the sun is warming you. You feel safe and happy.)

The tree starts to bud and the warmth of the sun helps the buds to flower. (*What would it feel like to flower?*) The flowers turn into leaves. The tree is now feeling alive again and is ready to continue it's growth.

You are now free to let your tree grow, but remember you are not in a hurry, a tree just grows and grows without questioning and without judgment. Feel the freedom you have as the tree gets bigger and bigger until one day you actually meet the tree like an old friend. You walk around it and you rub your hand on its bark and say hello. The tree welcomes you and you step inside for the first time.

(Picture yourself walking up to the tree for the first time, this meditation has now come full circle and it is a wonderful thing.)

The power of this mediation is very special because you have to just trust that the right things are going to happen. You learn to let go of control and just feel and not question. Often in life when we feel emotion, we try to fight that feeling instead of trying to accept it. This is a valuable lesson, because we must feel all emotion. It doesn't matter if it's the good, the bad, or the ugly, it is okay to feel it all. Accept it all and know that everything in life will pass if we allow it to. Life will carry on (just like the tree will continue to grow everyday) and so will you. Giving yourself the power to let go is taking control, and trusting is a sign of strength.

Allow this meditation to grow inside you, let it become part of your tree meditation like I have for my safe place. A backstory and a history of strength that you can draw upon in your everyday life, make this meditation mean more and be even more special to you and you alone. This meditation surely proves just how powerful your mind can be.

Using Meditation as a Healing and Therapeutic Tool

The concept of using meditation as a healing tool was introduced to me when I was in therapy for depression, to help me learn how to let go of the negative emotions and negative situations that had happened to me and still controlled how I felt about myself and who I was. I had allowed these emotions and situations to controlled my self-esteem, keeping me trapped in the past and unable to move forward in my life.

Using meditation to change these emotions and situations was a powerful gift. When you use meditation in this way you take the situation that happened and you resolve it in a natural way, a way that is comfortable and special to you. I would like to share a mediation that was given to me in therapy called "The Glass House." I use this glass house meditation in three different ways. I will walk you through the first way and then I will also give examples of two other personal meditations I came up with to heal past events and negative situations that occur in life. All three of these meditations are very powerful and fulfilling. You will then have the power to make them your own and use them as you feel you need to.

The following meditation worked wonders for me, and I was able to close out many longstanding problems that were still impacting me in my every-day life. I feel the only way to change a negative experience that has caused trauma in your life is to counter it with a positive one- one that clears out the negative situation and replaces it with a positive one. In doing so you now have a new memory and a new experience that is far more powerful and positive than the original. What makes it so powerful is the fact that you created it yourself and you truly believe it in your mind, body and soul. We cannot control what may happen to us at the hands of others, but we can make an outcome for ourselves that is positive and allows us to move forward in a health way. This helps us heal the past and paves the way for a happy and bright future.

After the Glass House we will look at two other meditations that are extensions of the glass house, building on the same environment.

The Glass House meditation is a special meditation, a place to clear out negative emotion and situations that have been hurting you and replace them with positive ones.

This is how it works: you go to the glass house in your mind, and it can be any type of house, big, small, it doesn't matter. It can be anywhere you wish it to be, you are in control of what it looks like and where it is, which is part of it being so therapeutic because you make it personal and unique to what will be relaxing for you specifically.

What happens in the house is truly special. Once you are in the glass house you will see that there is a wonderful kitchen with a massive sink and high-pressure washer hanging above it. There are these dirt glass jars that are filled with negative emotions and there are labels on the front of every bottle. These labels are the negative emotions that you have and you want to change in your life. Hate, guilt, humiliation etc. The idea is that you take that dirty jar and you empty it out and scrub it clean, making sure that it is totally free from all dirt, which represents the negative emotion.

Then you reach over to the tap, which has ice cold spring water coming out of it, and you fill the jar. Then take the label off the jar and replace it with a new one, a new emotion, a positive emotion. You then take a long drink of this water and you allow it to fill your body with the new emotion. You become that emotion and kill off the negative one that was once in the jar. Then take the jar and place it on a shelf with other jars you have done the same procedure to already.

You keep these jars on the shelf in plain view so you can see them every time you visit the glass house. You may even drink from them again and fill yourself up with that positive emotion if you need to. You can visit this glass house anytime you'd like, it is a safe place like my tree or whatever your safe place is. You are in a place where you are free to feel and deal with anything in your life or just go and relax. You are always free to just look at the jars and feel proud of yourself for what you have accomplished in the past.

This meditation is very therapeutic in many ways. When you are washing out the jar you are physically washing way a situation in your life that caused you to feel negative emotions. The act of cleaning is the act of taking away the power it had over you and then replacing it with a new emotion you want to believe is alive in you. The water is black and negative so you pour it down the drain and you empty yourself of the negative emotion.

You put a new label on the bottle that is positive, one that you want to believe about yourself. You drink the water and you allow yourself to feel the positive emotion and energy. You believe this change has happened inside of you because you have taken it into your body and in doing so you fully believe it and accept it. You take the time to allow the cold, clear water to fill you with that emotion, you feel it in your body and allow it to become real. This can now feel like a physical thing that has happen to you.

The bottles are always kept on a shelf like trophies you have earned, as proof of what you have accomplished. Not only that but you are welcome to drink from them anytime to replenish these positive feelings and emotions when you feel you need to. These bottles become a recourse to you and you can go to the glass house any time you need to fill your body with the strength and happiness that is in each one.

Below is an excerpt from my book "Why I Run" where I used the glass house as a way to close out an EMDR session, where I learned to change failure to success. After you read this excerpt, I will share with you my glass house meditation.

When I finally finished proving myself wrong over and over again I went to my safe place and just thought of nothing but taking in air through my leaves and out through my roots. I stayed in the tree till I felt I was ready, and then I did the last thing I needed to do.

I have a house we go to sometimes to help close out the therapy sessions. It's a meditation exercise. A glass house sits in the middle of a beautiful, green grass field surrounded by a forest of tall trees.

This house is a peaceful place. It is a laboratory where some large bottles with water in them are kept. They are all labeled with words that represent my emotions, good and bad. I take the bad emotion that I am dealing with and I empty out that bottle and I wash it up and I fill it with clean water. I put a new label on it and take a nice long drink from it, letting this new emotion fill me up. Then I place this new bottle on a clean shelf with the other bottles that I have done the same with. I like to sit in an office chair and look out at the forest until I am at peace. Then I open my eyes and I am free.

This time I had something special for the bottle, a feeling called failure. That bottle had been hidden for so long. I took it and emptied its black, dirty water down the drain, but then I did something different with it. This time I placed that bottle in the garbage. I had no use for it anymore. It was time to just say goodbye. I didn't even want to reuse it as a container for the new emotion. I asked Mastora if I could just get a new bottle and label it success and she said, "Of course you can." So I walked over to the closet and opened the door and there were hundreds of new, clean bottles for me to fill!! I took one and put the label on and wrote "Success" on it. I filled it up and drank from it and I cried. I know I am not a failure. Never was, never will be.

I walked over to the office chair and I smiled with joy. I sat there peacefully. Mastora asked how much I still believed I was a failure after this EMDR. I told her, "Zero." She asked me, when I think of these police and RCMP tests now, what do I feel? I told her I feel strong and I feel smart and I feel these feelings in my heart to be 100% true. I opened my eyes and I am free from failure.

Glass House

Close your eyes and breathe deeply and slowly, feel each breath and how it moves in through your nose, into your lungs, and feel your chest rise and then fall as you exhale. Feel each breath fully, noticing more about each one as you slowly and complete relax.

When you are ready, picture yourself walking down a path through a forest. At the end of the path there is an opening which leads to a wild green field with manicured grass.

(Picture this green field, bringing in all your senses that we have been working on. What do you see, hear, smell, etc. as you walk down this path?)

The green field is sounded by larger trees and at the far right side of this field is a glass two storey house. You know this house is magic because as you walk closer to it, you can tell that it is glass but you are unable to see inside or through it. The glass is foggy, as if there is smoke trapped in it. As you walk closer you notice there are wonderful rose gardens on either side of the stone walkway leading up to the front door. There are three stairs leading to the front door with silver hand rails on either side of the stairs and a red front door.

(Breathe deeply now and really picture this magical house. Take your time and look at the rose bushes, really see the flowers. What colour are they? Feel free to stand there and see it all for yourself as if you are truly there, even walk over to the roses and smell them if you'd like,)

The stone path leads you around the right side of the house. As you turn there is a lattice work wall, covered with honeysuckle vine. The vine is thick and has created a wall of green leaves and white and yellow flowers. The sight of this wall is unreal and the smell is intoxicating. On your left side there is a solid green hedge that is trimmed to perfection, about one foot high.

(See this now as you walk down this path to the back of the house, smell the rich honeysuckle vine as you walk. Take your left hand and run it over the green hedge, feeling the soft green leaves' new growth and energy.)

As you enter the backyard you pass through an arch way which is covered with that same honeysuckle vine. The first thing you see is a sunken fire pit with wicker patio furniture placed around it. There are a few burnt logs in the pit from a late night fire you had enjoyed on a different trip to the house.

(What does this fire pit look like? Can you smell the burnt logs? What does the furniture look like? Make this fire pit the way you want it to be.)

You pass by the fire pit and see there is a large rectangular in-ground pool with magical sky blue water. The pool is surrounded with red Japanese maple trees. You have gone swimming in this pool many times. The pool's water is very warm and welcoming.

(Take the time and picture this pool. Imagine swimming in it... imagine how warm the water is as you slowly walk down the stairs into the pool and your body becomes surrounded by its warmth. Feel free to stay in this moment as long as you'd wish.)

You look over your shoulder and follow the path up to the back of the house. There is a stairway leading to the back door with silver hand rails just like the one at the front of the house. You walk up the stairs and there is a large sliding glass door. To the left of the door there is a hand sensor which you place your left hand on and the door magically slides open for you to enter.

(What does the back of the house look like? Get a good look before you walk up the stairs. Is there a garden, maybe a pond that you'd like to sit beside and watch fish swim? See it all, make this place yours! Add to the backyard as you see fit.)

You walk into the house and there is living room to your right with a sofa and a love seat. There are wonderful hand painted pictures on the walls, and the floors are natural coloured hard wood. There is a very calm feeling in the house; a feeling of comfort, a feeling of being safe.

(Picture this living room as you walk into it. The room can be any colour you wish, the furniture and style any way you want it to be. The paintings can be what you want them to be, what you smell, hear is all up to you as this is your glass house.)

You walk through the living room and into the next room. This room is the laboratory where you wash out the dirty bottles filled with the negative emotions you have carried with you for so long. There is a large metal industrial sink with a high-pressure washing hose hanging down over it. There is also a shelf above the sink which has a bunch of bottles labelled with the names of positive emotions and filled with clear, clean water.

(Imagine you are looking at this laboratory and try to see every detail, from what the sink looks like to how many bottles are on the shelf. What labels can you see from where you're standing and how does it feel when you read them, seeing that you have overcome so much already? Or is that shelf empty and you are getting a fresh start today?)

You walk over to the sink and on the floor is a dirty bottle with a negative emotion written on it.

(What is this emotion that is sitting there in front of you? Make it your own, what would you like to change it to?)

You reach down and lift the bottle up to the sink, carefully twist the top off the large bottle, then empty the dirty liquid down the drain.

(Watch as you empty this bottle of its horrible dark liquid. How does it feel to finally just pour this negativity down the drain? Let the feeling of freedom fill your body, feel it deep in your soul like you are purging this emotion out of yourself, becoming free of its grip.)

Once the bottle is empty, take the pressure washer and clean out the remainder of the dirty liquid. Wash off the dirt that is clinging to the sides of the jar. Make sure you wash it all off and this bottle is completely free of the old negative emotion that was previously in there for so long.

(Picture washing way the dirt from the sides, take your time and get it totally clean.)

After you are finished washing away the dirt and grime from inside the bottle, take it over to the tap that is just a few steps away and turn on the tap. The water coming out of the tap is the purest water you can drink and it is cold as ice. You fill the bottle to the top and walk back over to where the lid of the bottle is resting on the counter. You place the jar down gently and pull open the drawer just below the sink's counter top. In this drawer there are white labels and a Sharpie magic marker. You take one of the labels and stick it to the jar. You then write the positive emotion you want to fill yourself with on the label with your Sharpie.

(Write the positive emotion on the bottle and make it mean something, make sure that it is truly what you wish to feel.)

Now that the bottle is labelled, grab it with both hands and raise it up to your mouth. Take a drink of the water. The cold water enters your mouth and moves down your throat. Let it fill you with the positive emotion. Breathe deeply and imagine that it is filling you up from the bottom of your feet all the way up through your body. You feel this new emotion fill you right to the tips of your fingers, all the way up to the top of your head.

(Take the time now to fully feel this magic water fill your entire body, let yourself go and imagine just what it feels like to completely, without question accept this new feeling and believe it to be true.)

Once you have drank the clean water/emotion and have truly felt it in your body and accepted it, put the bottle down and put the lid back on it. Now lift it and place it on top of the shelf with the others. Walk over to the office chair that is behind you and sit down. Look at the bottles that you have in front of you. *(Take the time now to look at the bottles- what do they look like? Are they all the same shape, or are some bigger than others? As you look at each bottle, feel the pride at completing this task wash through your body. You have changed your emotional state and the bottles/bottle is the proof.)*

You sit there for the moment and relish the experience. You just accomplished a great task! You got rid of a negative emotion you felt about yourself and replaced it with a positive one, and this is something you should be proud of! After a short while you get up from the chair and walk out of the laboratory and into the living room. You pass through the living room and make your way to the door. You place your hand on the sensor and as the door opens for you to walk through, you look back over your shoulder and take one last, long look at the inside of the house.

(Make sure as you walk out of the house that you see everything as if you are truly there, you take a good look and picture the inside of your glass house, burn it into your mind and memory to make it as real as you can.)

You now walk down the stairs and have a good look at the backyard, including the pool, the fire pit, and the lush gardens. As you walk down the path you once again smell the honeysuckle vine and pass through the arch towards the front of the house. You take a moment to pause and stare up at the house before you walk back through the green field to the secret path in the woods that will lead to your car.

(Truly see this world as you walk out of it; hear and smell every thing that you can around you, because this is your private place. This is where your glass house is.)

As you make your way to where your car is parked, take the time to truly embrace the positive feeling you have and remember how good it felt to fill your body with this emotion as you drank from the bottle. The negative emotion is gone and you are now free from it. Walk up to your car, get in, and drive away.

The glass house is a meditation that you are free to use anytime you'd like. You are also free to go back to the house and just relax, make it a safe place for you to escape to whenever necessary. You can also drink from the bottles anytime you need to revitalize yourself with the positive emotions contained there.

I have used this glass house meditation in different ways- to heal old traumas, even sometimes to rebuild my self confidence after a particularly hard day. I will go to the glass house when I am feeling overwhelmed, look at the bottles (even drink from them) and feel each emotion, each feeling and leave fully recharged.

I would like to now share with you the other meditations that I have created and put into practice as I have turned the glass house meditation into a special place, a place of healing, a place where I am free to use different techniques to better myself and find peace. The goal is to let your mind completely be free and use as much creativity as you would like. You can create your own variations on what I am about to share, or make up your own from scratch as well.

The Pool

The pool in the glass house meditation is a magic pool, and I have often used this pool to wash away a bad situation that caused me to feel upset or uncomfortable. I have used it after a bad day at work to completely wash away the day so I can relax and unwind and be free.

I have also gone there for a swim halfway through my day just a treat, a way to celebrate and indulge myself in a wonderful experience.

I go to the glass house as always, starting the meditation the same way. I picture myself once again walking to the glass house, going around back, walking up to the pool and then taking off my clothes and slowly walking into the pool.

As I walked down into the water, I would truly go back to the situation that was still causing me pain and I would remember everything about what happened: the emotions I felt, what I saw, smelled, anything that would truly bring me back to that situation. Then as I stepped down into the water I would imagine that the water is magic and that it has the power to wash this situation and the emotions which were attached to it away from my body. The water cleanses my whole being from bottom to top.

As I go deeper and deeper into the pool, the negative emotion is washed away. I get deep enough in the water to where I can finally dive forward and swim, so I go under the water completely and wash myself clean of the negative feeling, cleansing my mind, body and soul.

I like to swim in the pool and truly feel the freedom that is created by this action. I replace the bad memories that were associated with any situation with the feeling of being washed free from it, focusing on how good it feels to swim around in this pool, this freedom. I truly feel the new positive emotions and close out the bad.

From that point I make a bridge between the old memory and the new, so if that situation comes back into my mind again I remember washing it away in the pool and the negative emotion would no longer affect me in the way it did before. I take power away from the negativity and replace it with the feeling of being free, I take pride in having this ability and I carry that with me as well.

When something happens to us it is real, and it makes us feel a certain way. A true to life physical thing that happened can dominate our lives. When we meditate we can counter that negative physical action with our own action, making it real for ourselves. This is what using meditation as a therapeutic tool is all about.

Once I am done swimming I walk out of the pool and dry off with a nice, fluffy, soft towel that is waiting for me at the side of the pool. I put on a warm house coat. I then like sit in a chair and look out into the wonderful forest that is behind the pool. Taking in the surroundings, I use all my senses and make the glass house a truly relaxing place.

I like to sit and feel very proud of what I just accomplished by washing myself free of the negative and making myself truly free.

I like to do this because when you are so unaccustomed to feeling pride and positive emotion it often feels very uncomfortable and unnatural. So the more time you spend feeling these emotions, the easier it becomes to feel them without guilt, and this will transfer into your outside life because of this meditation.

After you sit for a while, get dressed and take your time walking out of the back yard. As you do, truly feel all the positive emotions you have just given yourself. List them in your mind or even out loud if you'd like as you walk back to where you entered and finish your trip to the glass house the same way you started it.

The Fire Pit

I created the fire pit behind the glass house during a therapy session where I was working on my self esteem. I had so many instances in my life where I felt that I just did not measure up, I had failed at so many things and I thought very little of myself. I wanted to clear all of this out and to really get rid of these past situations because they were holding me back from being who I wanted be. They had shaped my life for too long and I placed too much value on them. I wanted to feel good about myself and be happy. I was in therapy for depression and it was working wonders, and since I was progressing and moving forward with my life it was finally time to resolve and heal these past events.

I went to the glass house and I stood at the counter, looking at the jar that was filled with the horrible dark liquid with the label "useless" written on it. I decided to do something different. I got a pen and a stack of paper out of a drawer under the sink and I started to write out each instance that had impacted my life.

I wrote about times when I felt humiliated, ashamed, worthless- you name it, I wrote about. I wrote freely and without a second thought. I gave every single situation that I had floating around in my mind and all the past situations that haunted me on daily basis the time they deserved. I wrote and didn't pull any punches. Whether they were small or not, I wrote about every single detail.

When I was finished writing I grabbed this pile of paper and I headed outside. I walked over to the fire pit and took my time placing some wood in the pit along with old, used newspapers. After striking a match and letting the newspaper catch, I had built a nice sized fire. When it was just the right size, I walked over to the fire with my papers in hand. I slowly crumpled each paper up into a ball, one at a time, and threw them into the fire. As I threw each paper into the fire I watched as they went up in flame, each one disappearing, turning to ash. I took a deep breath with each one and truly said goodbye to each experience that haunted me. I was filled with relief as I did this, because I knew I had no more time in my life to waste on these old skeletons that kept rattling around in my closet. As much as I loved saying goodbye I also realized that all these situations molded me over time, and I would not be where I am right now without them. Coming to grips with that was hard because I hated those times in my life for so long but I had to finally let go and be free. Holding on to bad things in life just never works out and you have to say goodbye and move forward, learn from your past and be better because of it.

After I was finished I then walked back into the glass house, emptied that glass jar labeled "useless" and cleaned it thoroughly, making sure all the negative was truly gone and washed way. I then filled it with cold, clear water from the tap and took a long drink. I let myself truly feel free and strong, filled with confidence! I put a new label on that jar and I wrote "successful and strong" on it.

Afterwards I went outside to the fire pit and sat in the comfy chair, watching the fire burn into the night. As I sat there, I allowed myself to feel confident, I allowed myself to feel happy and successful. I took the time to feel these feelings in my heart and I paid attention to how my body was feeling, how I was lighter than air. I also really paid attention to how I truly believed this positivity in my mind, body and soul.

After I was finished this meditation I took the time to leave the same way I had come in.

The fire pit is a very power meditation because it allows you to fully confront the situation from your past, write it out and fully remember it, give it the time it deserves, and then burn it and make it disappear. Creating an actual action to counter the original situation that happened in your life is the most important thing above all. It creates closure and truly sets you free. You remember that you dealt with the situation and give yourself the chance to move forward but you close this chapter in a way that is final and you are comfortable with it. Then when you go back into the glass house you empty the jar, wash it out and drink the cold water, filling yourself with the new positive emotion.

This meditation could have many different therapeutic directions, but it is up to you to come up with your own ways of using it and making it a safe place where you truly heal and enjoy your time.

Whether it is to clear out a trauma or to just enjoy yourself, the glass house can be a starting point to many meditations you can create for yourself. It is very important to have a place you can always fall back on when meditating, a place that is familiar and that you can easily get to in your mind because sometimes it is not easy to reach a meditative state, to focus you mind.

I hope that these glass house meditations have given you a direction to follow, to create your own glass house meditations, clear out old traumas, and help you build a stronger and more confident you!

The garden in the woods is yet another healing meditation where I took a physical activity and turned it into a meditation. Mixing something I love to do with clearing my mind and enjoying a rich experience (and also healing and feeling good about myself!) is easy to do when you've created a guided meditation using all of your senses.

In my first book, I wrote about enjoying gardening and how I drew on the similarities between cutting back the overgrown bushes and changing my life and my way of thinking. Below is an excerpt from "Why I Run".

I had a coffee on my back porch and just relaxed. Then I worked in my front yard. I had cut back all the beautiful lavender bushes. Before that, they were huge and they all died from the long, hard winter we had. As I cut them back I thought about every cut I made. Each one was like me cutting back everything from my past and learning to let it go and make way for new growth, new life for the lavender and for me at the same time.

It may take years for the lavender to grow as big as it was but I don't care. I just let it grow and the same with me. I am learning so much. Sometimes I have good days and sometimes bad but I am getting there day by day, moment by moment.

I spent two hours out front working and enjoyed it all. Never a bad thought and never a thought about work, which normally by that point in the day would have got into my head. I would have called at least three times by now worried about inventory or something like that thinking that if I am not at work or having contact with work that something bad will happen. But I am learning to not take work home with me, that the work is not going anywhere and it will be there when I get back. Me worrying and calling is not going to change anything at the store. Learning to let go of things and not worry is turning out to be a very good thing. Something I have to let myself grow as well.

In the below meditation I drew on the gardening experience I wrote about in "Why I Run" and created another way of using meditation as a therapeutic tool.

The Secret Garden in the Woods

One morning while sitting on my yoga mat beside my pond, while breathing deeply, completely relaxed with my eyes closed and mind clear, I decided to go for a walk in the woods. This is the same forest that frames the open green field in my safe place and my glass house meditation. I wanted to create a magical place where I was free do something I loved – gardening – but I wanted to make it a very, very personal place. Read below and transport yourself there now with me as we go to the garden in the woods.

Walk down the path that leads through the forest from my tree, my safe place. As you walk along this path you look straight ahead and see the opening to the green field, then you look to your left and see a wall of thick pine trees with an almost unnoticeable path leading to it.

(Start the meditation the same way we started the safe place meditation and the glass house meditation. This is a familiar place, a place you have been before. Picture yourself walking down this path through the woods, towards the opening to the green field. Fully go there, take your time and enjoy the walk and when you ready, turn to your left and see the wall of pine trees.)

As you walk closer to the path, you notice that this is an illusion. This is a secret path through the pine trees, a secret passage through to a hidden place beyond.

(Imagine walking on this path and it slowly exposes itself to you. This is a path to a secret place, see and make this as real as you can.)

There is a zigzag cut out of the tree limbs, and as you entered you could smell the fresh sharp scent of pine. You make a turn to the left, then right, then left again. There is an arch way just up ahead of you made up of twisted vine and covered with yellow and white flowers. You walk towards this arch way and you can see nothing past the entrance; it is like a liquid mirror, and you only see yourself in the mirror.

(As you walk towards the entrance, what to you smell, how do you feel? Are you excited, or scared? Feel every emotion, think about how you would feel and then allow yourself to feel everything as if you were there.)

You take a deep breath and walk through the archway, and you are amazed at what is waiting on the other side. You are transported to a magical place! Straight in front of you is a massive pond, a 20 foot circle with a wall of rock framing the edges. There are five water spouts shooting water high into the air. At the back of the pond there is a slow running waterfall, the water gently running down and passing through the slick and mossy stones, landing with a calming splash in the water below.

(See this pond and use everything you have learned about bringing in all your senses to really travel to this hidden place. What do you see, hear, smell, feel? Use every tool you have and see this magical place.)

There are yellow water lilies floating in the pond. As you walk closer, stop to watch the goldfish swimming under the cover of large lily pads. The goldfish are fast and they race each other through the water. The fish are not too big, only about 5 to 6 inches long, but they are the most vibrant orange you have ever seen.

There is a path around the pond on both sides, and each side is framed by a larger stone wall covered with honeysuckle vine, yellow and white flowers in full bloom. You can smell the sweet scent as you walk around the pond.

The path around the pond is paved with well worn cobblestone and covered with green moss that almost seems to glow. You walk to the left of the pond and noticed that there is a large garden behind the waterfall.

(Now as you walk past the pond, see all the detail, smell the honeysuckle vine, feel the mossy rocks under your feet as you walk around the pond.)

There are raised planter boxes, rows and rows of them as far as your eyes can see. You walk forward into the garden and off to your right side you see there are watering cans, gardening gloves, waste paper bags, garden tools and a hand pump for water just up against the wall.

(What does this little work station look like? Is there a shed there, maybe a work bench? See this and make it real.)

You move forward and see that five of the planters have been weeded and well cared for. You walk over to the work station and take some gloves, a paper bag for waste, a hand cultivator and a small shovel. You walk over to a planter box that has not yet been weeded.

(See this planter box, the wood it is made from, and the plants that are within it – they can be any type you'd like.)

As you stand in front of the planter box, you pull the gloves on. (*Alternatively, you could leave the gloves off and get a feel for the dirt and weeds you are now going to touch with your hands.*) You then start pulling out weeds that are intertwined between the plants which are just starting to take bloom.

(What do the flowers look like on the plants you are weeding around? See them and stop the work to bend over and smell them, make this experience a slow and enjoyable task.

Take the time as you pull out each weed to think about your actions, and feel good about freeing the plants from the weeds castrates. You are now freeing yourself at the same time, letting go of your stresses and being proactive as you do so. You are pulling out these weeds and freeing the plants to grow and flower.)

The soil is rich and black, and you carefully pull the weeds out. You can smell the dampness of the soil and it is soft to the touch. You work your way around the one side of the planter and place the weeds into the paper bag.

(Feel the freedom of placing the unwanted weeds in the trash.)

You work your way to the other side and start pulling out the weeds. *(Concentrate on the job at hand, nothing else; each weed is special and needs your full attention.)* Work your way to the end of the planter and again place the waste in the paper bag.

Take a walk around the planter now and have a good look, making sure you have got all the weeds that were growing and taking up the space that plants are now free to grow in. Once you are satisfied with your work, take the bag back to the place where you first got it from.

Now take the hand cultivator and gently fluff up the soil surrounding the plant. Work your way around the box, taking your time and making sure all the soil is turned over.

(Take your time and really see the fruits of your labour, picture the rich soil and maybe take some and hold it in your hand, breathe in the scent of the damp earth and enjoy this moment.)

Walk over to where the water pump is and take a watering can and place it under the pump. Grab the handle and begin to pump the handle up and down. After about the fifth pump the water explodes out of the end of the pump and fills the steel watering can. You carry the watering can over to the planter box and slowly tip the can. The water cascades out through the many holes and waters the rich soil below.

(See the water now, smell rich dirt as the water hits the soil and intensifies the scent.)

Take the time and work your way around the planter box, making sure that each plant gets it's fair share of water before walking back and placing the watering can back where it came from.

You stand and look at the planter box and feel good about the job you did weeding and caring for it. You turn and walk back towards the hand pump to wash your hands.

(You feel proud of yourself, your planter box looks amazing and you feel amazing as well!)

You turn and start walking back towards the pond and as you walk you breathe in deeply, exhale slowly letting the air just pass out smoothly from your lungs. You look at the wall of honeysuckle vine and make sure to once again take a massive inhale as deep as you can to experience the rich, sweet smell and enjoy it fully. You reach the side of the pond and stop. You watch the fish swim, listen to the stream of water calmly falling, then hitting the pond with a soft splash.

(*You are in no hurry to leave this place, empty your mind by truly seeing, hearing and smelling everything. Breathe deep and long, living in the moment you have created in your own mind.*)

After a while (when you are ready) slowly walk past the pond, through the magic vine arch way. Once again you are now walking through the wall of pine trees. You walk through the zigzag path cut out of those trees which keeps this place hidden from the world. You continue on down the path which lead you there. As you walk on the path, it eventually rejoins the original path that leads you in to the forest. You turn and although the wall of pine trees is there, the path leading to it slowly disappears before your eyes.

(*See the pines, and the path slowly disappears.*)

What a wonderplace the secret garden is, and you will be able to go there anytime you'd like as the path will always appear when you walk by it. You continue to walk to the end of the path where you had entered. When you are ready, open your eyes and end this meditation.

Throughout my day after doing this meditation I will occasionally just close my eyes and breath deep and remember how I felt while I was in the secret garden. I will try to remember scents and images and get lost in the moment again. Sometimes a good meditation like this one will give me days of peace while I am at work, or if a stressful situation happens and I feel that I have to care for myself I will bring back the feelings, the imagery all of it! The wonderful thing about guided meditation is that you can go back to these places any time you'd like.

The way in which you use this meditation can be very healing. You can imagine that the planter is your life and that clearing out the weeds is clearing out the bad things in your life, you give the situations the time they need and then pull them out. You free up that now open space for positive growth, and not only that but then you care for yourself. You cultivate the dirt and prepare it for new growth, you take the water and you feed the plant (yourself) giving it the life-giving gift of water. When the water hits the dirt, new things start to happen!

When you start to care for yourself and invest in your own healing and growth amazing things happen and soon you will flower and grow big and strong! Soon you will fill the new, empty space that was left when the bad weeds were cleared out with new growth. I love using physical examples of growth when healing and investing in my own health and well-being. We are all alive, just like a tree or a plant, and we all need to grow to become who we are meant to be.

Practice this secret garden meditation and make it your own, truly go there and cultivate new growth for yourself!

The Power of Written Word and Meditation

I would like to share an example of just how powerful our minds actually are, something showing that when this power is focused, we can accomplish great things. I will say this again because I firmly believe it, people who struggle with depression, anxiety, and any other mental illness are some of the most brilliant and smart people you will ever meet. Their minds are just working all the time. But they have never learned how to focus their overactive minds in a health way. For me, meditation has become the greatest outlet for my overactive mind, and I have used it for many, many different therapeutic experiences.

I have learned over the past five years of therapy to focus my overactive mind, and sometimes it is hard and sometimes it is easy. I learned that writing allows me to deal with so many things in my life because I can reason things out, see the world in different ways, create wonderful meditations, and have a safe place to go to in my mind.

I can also put pen to paper or fingers to a keyboard and use writing as a therapeutic tool. I have learned how to heal traumas in my life, to come up with solutions and find closure to life changing events. I started to practice this after doing EMDR therapy. I did this by going back over old traumas, reliving them, and in doing so taking the power back and finding my own solutions and closing them out.

This has been a game changer in my life, it has had such an impact on me that it inspired me to write "Creative Writing For The Mind, Body & Soul" so other people can learn what I have learned and in doing so making therapy a personal and wonderful experience. The only way therapy ever works is when you accept it and you learn to apply it in your own way, a way that you embrace and turn into something you enjoy doing (not something you have to do.)

If you can accomplish that then you are on your way to changing your life, and your future will be as bright as you wish it to be.

I am now going to share a very personal trauma that has been effecting me everyday since it happened: the death of my father. I remember I was doing a talk at Brock University shortly after my father had passed away, and a student asked a question that stopped me dead in my tracks. I was floored and almost started to cry in front of the entire class that I was speaking to. The question was, "Do you feel you are now cured from your depression?... seeing as you have written two books and are talking openly about it and teaching." I was hit so hard by this question. I realized at that point that I wasn't even close to cured, and I had no clue how to grieve for my father. I responded by saying that "I never look at it as being cured, that at different points in our lives we face different situations and those situations need the proper care and attention they deserve to prevent a slip in our emotion states". I then talked about losing my father and how I had gone from going to therapy once a month to going back to once a week, because I needed the help to deal with this new situation I had never face before.

Grieving for the loss of my father was the hardest thing I have faced in my life. After a year of therapy, I did something that I never thought I could do: I said goodbye to my father.

I am going to share how, through meshing written word with meditation, I was able to finally find some peace and say goodbye to him in my own personal way, a way that I created and felt comfortable with and have fully accepted.

Saying Goodbye to My Dad

This morning I thought about my dad, about how nice it would be to be with him again. If I could be with him again I would tell him about the wonderful things in my life. I would not waste any time asking him questions about the afterlife, but instead tell him about Dylan (my son). How he will be turning 11 soon, how big he is getting. I would love to see his smile and hear his voice, feel his spirit, calm and loving again. So I finally decided to go and see him.

I took deep breaths, I closed my eyes and I went to my safe place- my tree. I walked around my tree and I ran my hand over its bark saying hi and letting it know I was there. I took a deep breath and I stepped inside. I continued to breathe deeply, and I sat crossed legged in the trunk. I breathed deep and took air in through my leaves, down through the trunk, out through my roots and back again. I felt everything the tree could feel. I stayed there living in the moment until I built up the courage to see my dad. I stood up, I took a deep breath and I stepped out of the tree.

I was then in a large green field with small yellow flowers mixed in the green grass. This field was lit with a huge bright sun, framed by a deep blue sky with no clouds in sight. The field stretched out with no end, and there was a calming, cool breeze. About fifty feet in front of me were two leather arm chairs. My dad was sitting in the chair on the left-hand side. As I walked toward him he turned and smiled at me and said, "Hi Darc." He was no longer the man I watched die slowly, but he was now back to being the healthy, strong man I knew when I was just a little boy, a man in the prime of his life. His eyes were bluer then the sky and filled with happiness because he was going to get to sit and talk with me for the first time in almost a year. I said, "Hi, Dad" and sat down beside him.

I reach out and held his hand like I did when I was just a little boy. I let the feeling of being safe and happy fill me. We sat together and looked out at the vast green field in front of us, feeling each other's presence, the love we have for each other. I squeezed my dad's hand and he turned to look at me with a big smile. I said, "I miss you so much, every day" and he replied "I miss you too." I then told him that I am having a very hard time with losing him, I miss him everyday. My dad smiled and said he misses me as well and I need to let go and be happy again, live my life because that is what life is for, living. I then told him all about my books, the people I am helping, the lives that I am changing. He smiled and told me he always knew I was meant to do great things in life. I looked into his eyes and I smiled and said, "Thank you, Dad." I then told him about Dylan, how smart he is, how big he is getting and how good of a boy he is growing up to be.

My dad squeezed my hand and told me I am a wonderful father, Sherri (my wife) is a wonderful mother and that Dylan will grow up to be a great man because of us. I said thank you to my dad and we once again looked off into the distance together, just feeling the love we have for each other. I enjoyed the feeling of being in the presence of my hero, my Dad.

I took a long deep breath and said, "Dad, I need to say goodbye now, I need to let your death pass, I need to let go and feel the loss and start living my life again." My dad smiled and said, "Darcy, I am always with you, in your thoughts, in your heart, your soul." I replied and said "Everything about you lives in me, you were the greatest father anyone could have had."

He just smiled and said, "Thank you Darcy, I did the best I could, now go and live your life, I am always with you…"

We both stood up and we hugged for a long time. I let go of him and looked him in his beautiful blue eyes and told him I loved him, I loved him so much. He looked at me with his eyes watering and told me he loved me too.

I slowly walked away from my dad, my hero, the man who has influenced my life in so many ways. I said goodbye to him.. After a year of grieving in silence, fighting and fighting with myself over his death, I said goodbye. As I walked away towards my tree I turned and my dad was standing and waving goodbye to me. The same way he would when we would back out of his driveway after a Sunday afternoon visit. I waved back to him for the last time and continued to walk to my tree. The air was now warmer and I could feel my father's love for me now more than ever before. I turned back again and my dad was now sitting in the leather chair looking out into the vast green field. My heart was pounding and my throat was swollen unable to swallow, and I cried and cried as I walked closer to my tree. I had to say goodbye, I couldn't keep living the way I was living. My dad will always be in my heart and soul, in my thoughts when I need him. But I had to say goodbye because I am not meant to live my life being sad, holding onto sadness is not healthy, it is not what my father would want me to do. So I said goodbye in the only way that I could handle and accept.

I walked to my tree, I walked around it feeling the bark and I looked back one more time. There was a flash of light, a shooting star leaving the earth, and it was my dad. The leather chairs were gone and so was he. I stepped into my tree and I crossed my legs and I sat breathing deep in through my leaves, down through my trunk, out through my roots and back again, feeling everything the tree felt. I stayed there for a long time breathing deeply and truly being the tree. Once I was calm and at peace I stood up and stepped out of the tree.

I had to say good bye, and I knew that the only way I could do it was with this new tool I had embraced. Meshing writing with meditation and coming up with my own personal way of saying goodbye. I thought for a long time that I could deal with my dad's passing like everyone else, but I am not like everyone else, and there is no normal or right thing to do when you lose someone you love so much. There is no normal way of grieving and learning to live without someone.

My mind doesn't shut down and that power I have must be used, so I used it over a 24 hour time period to create this meditation to help me say goodbye to the most amazing, caring, loving person who gave me life and has had the largest influence on me. This was not an easy task and it trained me to my core, but I did it, as hard as it was to do I finally said goodbye to my dad and I am happy that I was able to. I love you Dad, I will see you again sometime!

I am happy that I was able to bring myself to this point in time, that I was able to look inside myself and pinpoint this emotional struggle that has been holding me back for a year. I am happy that I found a way to go and be with my dad, feel his love and say goodbye in a manner that suited me.

I didn't want to say goodbye for so long because I thought if I did it would mean that I didn't love my dad, that I would be a terrible son, a bad human being, but it is okay. My father gave me life and he would not want me to stop living after he passed. The same way I would not want Dylan to stop living after I pass. I had allowed negative thoughts, feelings and emotions, sadness, guilt, and anger control me since my dad's death. I have had great success helping people and changing their lives and the way they deal with emotion, but I never gave myself the same treatment I give others, the same love.

I write about it, I talk about it, but I never did it for myself when it came to my own dad's death. I am at peace now because I found this way to say goodbye. I will have ups and downs because I am human, but I take pride in what I have done. Goodbye Dad, I love you and I miss you!

This is how I mesh writing with meditation. I create the environment I want to be in and while I write, I let my mind truly go there. Writing out my meditation allows me to elevate the experience and allows me to reach a deeper state to heal and move forward. Meshing writing with meditation is truly a super power. I knew what I wanted to say to my dad and how I wanted it to end. It was very emotional and painful, but I did and now I am at peace with the loss. When you write you are in a safe place where you are able to express yourself in any manner you choose. Writing is a superpower, meditation is a superpower, and we all have it, we all have that overactive mind that craves to be focused and when it is we can all achieve great things. We can even heal that which we think is impossible to heal.

The Power of Meditation

The power of the mind is truly incredible! From the start of this book, we slowly learned to focus our minds, slowly walking our way through meditations, learning to use all of our senses. We learned that reaching a meditative state isn't an impossible task and hopefully put some misconceptions to rest. We learned how to be mindful, how to practice mindfulness, in our own ways. In learning to be mindful we got in tune with our emotions and how we feel and react. We felt the good emotions when we meditated, and when we finished a meditation, we learned to let them stay with us throughout the rest of our day. The bad emotions we simply let melt way as we truly enjoyed the meditative state we were able to reach.

Meditation is a superpower and like everything in life, we only get better at it with practice and then more practice. The act of practicing meditation is finding inner peace. Taking the time and putting your mind power to a good use is enjoyable and over time, that inner peace becomes a part of us. The inner peace that people who meditated often talk about reaching is what you experience. Learning to reach that point sometimes feels impossible until that one day when the light bulb goes off and you realize that you are reaching that state, that is one of the true powers of meditation, that as you grow in your practice the benefits grow as well.

My hope in writing this book was to slowly build the experiences, get you used to using your mind in new ways, and having you create your own images within each meditation. Learning to use meditation in a recreational manner. Truly enjoying the time in these special places and also having these meditations to use in ways you feel free to. Making meditation something you look forward to using on a daily basis. Mixing these experiences with physical movement, truly reaching a deep state of meditation in mind, body and soul is a wonderful experience.

Also, the power of carrying a meditation with you and making it part of your day is an incredible thing. Take the time to enjoy a meditation on your lunch break or at the halfway point in your day. But also to have it there when your day goes a little bad. Having an escape plan in place in your mind that is calm and welcoming is a helpful tool, learning to feel when you need to reflect on your emotional state and bring back the feelings you felt while you meditated is controlling your mind, body and soul.

Building your own safe place, truly centering and putting to use the power of your now focused mind to create a solid place to go to, a place to heal, to recover and feel safer then you ever felt before is a tool you can use to heal so many different situations. Having the freedom to make your own safe place has so much meaning. When you create the safe and you practice it regularly, you truly are using the power of your mind in ways that you never knew were possible before.

All of this was leading up to using meditation as a therapeutic tool. Learning that a physical action in your life can be countered by a physical action in your mind. That you can create healing environments and healing practices. The glass house is a true example of a healing environment where I created different ways of healing past events in my life and also created a place where I am truly free to be happy and reinforce the work I have done.

Meditation seemed like it was a waste of time for me when I started, but it has turned into the greatest gift. A gift that I cultivated and made my own over time, and that was the key. Like all the therapies I have been exposed to over the last five years, I had to learn to find a way to make it my own and when I did, I discovered that I enjoyed doing each therapy. The freedom I gave myself, the pride I felt as I took what was being given to me and turned it into something I loved is a feeling that is hard to describe.

That is the key and the main goal of this book! Practice every day, move at a speed you feel comfortable at, and never get discouraged. Enjoy your time meditating and creating wonderful experiences for yourself.

Most importantly, above all, realize that your overactive mind is a gift that just needs to be focused and you will find and create your own happiness! You will grow into the person you have always wanted to be!

"Only with open conversation can we break the stigma behind depression, let's start talking and do it together."

Darcy Patrick

CPSIA information can be obtained
at www.ICGtesting.com
Printed in the USA
LVHW111458140419
614105LV00001B/1/P